RICH & DYING

RICH

&

DYING

AN INSIDER
CALLS BULLSH*T
ON AMERICA'S
HEALTHCARE ECONOMY

JEB DUNKELBERGER

LIONCREST
PUBLISHING

RICH & DYING

An Insider Calls Bullsh*t on America's Healthcare Economy

ISBN   978-1-5445-2084-1 *Hardcover*
       978-1-5445-2083-4 *Paperback*
       978-1-5445-2082-7 *Ebook*

Dedicated to...

...the good men and women who work in the health insurance industry, know there's a better way, and are trying to find it. You will see the day!

...my tremendous family, including friends, siblings-in-law, step-siblings, half siblings, siblings, stepparents, in-laws, parents, my wife, and my God—thanks for giving the love, support, and courage I needed to take this on and see it through.

CONTENTS

INTRODUCTION

At the age of twenty-nine, I was named one of the young-est vice presidents in the history of the seventh-largest health insurance company in the country—so young that they had to rewrite the job description because I didn't have enough experience on paper to qualify. I was respon-sible for managing a cross-functional team architecting an enterprise-wide initiative to align patient and provider incentives around value-based care, which, to date, has saved more than one billion dollars in medical and phar-maceutical spending. This achievement required much of our matrixed enterprise, which made the success that much sweeter, and showcased just how powerful we could be as a unified force. In recognition of this achievement, I was named one of "30 Under 30" by the *Pittsburgh Business Times* and surrounded by many leaders from our enterprise as we celebrated at the awards banquet.

My career was flying high.

I'd never felt worse in my professional life.

In hindsight, the value-based initiatives I led were essentially Band-Aids for a metastasizing tumor. Sexy, shiny little Band-Aids, but Band-Aids nonetheless—just one in a long line of industry self-reforms that have essentially failed to address the cancer at its source.

The results were great for the company. That year—and the year after and the year after that—were banner financial years, supported by initiatives like the one I led. Our profits ran in the hundreds of millions in each of those years.

We were a well-oiled machine led by some of the industry's brightest minds. We reinvested our margins back into the machine, using that money to buy or partner with strategic health systems, digitize many archaic and manual systems, invest in alternative revenue streams, and truly double down on our differentiators, fortifying our position as a dominant market player.

We weren't alone in this. Health insurers across the country have been operating in this fashion for years. And don't get me wrong; it wasn't a *bad* thing. We would employ more people, serve more patients, modernize patient and provider experiences, and increase access in more geographies as we grew. We had righteous goals to improve the quality of care, increase preventive services, address social determinants of health, and negotiate the most competitive value-based reimbursement rates with our providers—after all, a healthier and cheaper beneficiary is good for business!

But did the tangible value we created truly warrant those banner financial years? Did we actually see the needle move on delivering higher quality care at an affordable price?

I didn't see it, and I had a pit in my stomach that I couldn't shake. I came to a realization that I believe many noble people in the industry reach years later than I did, often when they've grown too settled and too comfortable to rock the boat. We all know the saying "Don't bite the hand that feeds you." Age and breadth of experience often bring wisdom and enlightenment, but that also comes with a family, a mortgage, and other daily comforts that are dependent on the status quo and create little incentive to truly reshape the system at its very foundation.

That's exactly where we have to begin—at the foundation.

I used to joke that I was just one date away from marrying a woman in Pittsburgh, buying a home, and aging comfortably, turning into another senior executive who won't be around long enough to see the system into its next chapter anyways.

As you may have already guessed, I didn't meet that woman in Pittsburgh. So I'm here to rock the boat. I know I'm not alone in my thinking; perhaps you have a pit in your stomach too. I hope what I have to say will encourage you to take a leap of faith and join me in rocking the boat.

THE SYSTEM ISN'T BROKEN

We've created a booming subindustry within healthcare dedicated to fixing the broken system. Everywhere you look, there are jobs and careers popping up around "fixing the problem." Shit, this book will join a litany of other publications focused on this exact topic—although I have an idea on how to make it different.

The thing is, there's a catch; it's not really a broken system. It's the *perfect* system—a system reacting perfectly to the market forces at play, human-made forces that are contributing to much of our nation's economic stability. It's even been described as recession-proof, with really only one thing capable of slowing it down: a global pandemic. Even so, as the pandemic passes, I predict growth will return in short order. In fact, the pandemic has ignited new arenas of digital and virtual health, which will amplify new verticals for spending and investment.

That said, I also think our *perfect* system has a hard-to-digest fixed variable: we need to keep spending at a high level on healthcare, because if we don't, our economy simply won't grow. It's like a bizarre form of Keynesian economics: put money in healthcare and watch the country's entire economic machine come to life. The healthcare sector is the country's largest employer. In order for our economy to survive, we need healthcare to employ millions upon millions of people. It's a machine that feeds off our economy while simultaneously driving it forward. (Perhaps Hank Paulson, the treasury secretary who gave us "too big to fail," should have figured this out back in 2008—but I digress.)

People need jobs, and healthcare provides great ones. But it is still a healthcare system, which must also deliver affordable, high-quality care. That's where the breakdown begins. The system we've built can't deliver that. In broad strokes, it is not efficient, it is not affordable, and it certainly isn't high quality.

I'm not going to talk about the "broken" system in this book. It's the perfect system, given what it's structured to produce. I want to reframe the conversation. I hope to help you look at the system's issues in a new light, because that will make you think differently about the needed next steps.

Think of it as a house with an unstable foundation. I don't care if you move the sofa from one side of the living room to the other. I don't care if you install a new roof, solar panels, or even a state-of-the-art home security system. The foundation is faulty; nothing else matters until that is resolved.

Talk of reform tends to point at physicians, hospital systems, or (you guessed it) pharmaceutical companies, because we think of them together as healthcare. Instead, I'm going to focus on the economy that's governing the system, which is the work of the health insurance industry.

This is not often talked about, and for a good reason. It's convoluted, hard to follow, and simply not that sexy. There are no *Grey's Anatomy* prime-time dramas featuring health insurance executives. The multibillion-dollar insurance lawsuits the industry generates don't often make it beyond trade journals and websites. And when they do make the front page of the newspaper, no one can make sense of it. What average American knows what it means to artificially inflate an RAF score?

Only our inner nerds can solve this problem. We need to hone in on the health insurance industry because it's where the money comes from, once it's been extracted from individuals, the federal government, and employers who purchase coverage for their employees and their dependents. The single largest block of insured Americans—over 180 million people—gets coverage through an employer-based benefit.

The vast remainder gain coverage through the federal government, but let's be honest, more times than not, these federal lines of business are publicly counted as loss leaders by providers, with much of a provider's margins cross-subsidized from commercial rates. That is not to say that an efficient provider *can't* remain solvent on Medicare rates. I've seen firsthand how efficiently a health system *can* be run, and commercial cross-subsidization is certainly not required; unfortunately this is still the exception and not the rule. This leaves employers paying for Medicare benefits twice: once through taxes and again through the cross-subsidy required to cover the government's underpayment. It's simply not sustainable. We're bound for collapse.

In the chapters to come, I'll be deliberate and detailed in examining the insurance system as it exists now and the reasons efforts to reform from within have failed. I'll examine the two poles of the political debate—the free-market approach from the right, the Medicare-for-all approach from the left—and explain why neither offers the answers we need. I'll review the insurance industry's efforts at self-reform and why they've fallen short. I'll acknowledge the realities that a new system must incorporate, then identify its core elements as well as the levers that might set it in motion.

Can we have both? A job-creating economic engine that also delivers affordable care at a higher quality?

I believe so. In fact, I already see signs of meaningful change here and there. But we can't just wait it out in our collapsing structure. We need to begin building a *new* system—right next to the one we've already got.

BECOMING A BOAT-ROCKER

I first experienced the healthcare industry from the patient's point of view. When I was ten, my stepmother was diagnosed with brain cancer. At sixteen, we learned she was terminal. Her treatments over those six years cost around $2 million (or $3.1 million in today's dollars), split between my family and our insurance carriers. Despite all that money and all that effort, she was dying anyway.

I'm not pointing fingers or saying it could have been avoided, but that's when I began to ask the question: Is this system living up to its potential?

After my undergrad years at Virginia Tech, I moved to the United Kingdom and attended the London School of Economics and Political Science, where I wrote a dissertation on the financial future of managed healthcare in America. I owe a great deal to my LSE professor and advisor, Dr. Adam Oliver, who convinced me that my original thesis plan, to explore the realities of Singapore's government-sponsored health system, was a blatant excuse to live in Southeast Asia for three months. He was not only correct, but he aligned me to the career I have today.

Ironically enough, I lived under a single-payer system as I wrote my dissertation, which was focused on my financial analysis of value-based incentives and patient cost sharing. One day, what I thought was a toothache turned out to be a head-wrenching sinus issue. I got a physician consult, X-ray, and medication on the day the pain began—no waiting and, even better, no bill.

I'm not saying the UK's National Health Service is the answer. But again, I asked the question: Is there a better way?

Shortly after completing my dissertation, I began my career as a management consultant in New York City. My first client was one of the largest insurance companies in the country. What I saw behind the curtain of the multibillion-dollar margins was a wacky, convoluted, manual, and highly inefficient workflow. I was focused in a claims processing division, where nearly 80 percent of claims were autoprocessed, yet the amount of inefficiency was still mind-boggling. If Debbie wasn't working on Monday, then her batch of claims didn't get processed; if Dr. Jones wasn't working on Tuesday, that prior authorization waited for his return; if Timmy needed to reconcile a provider contract, then he needed to call Annie, who would check a binder from ten years ago to find the signed document. At a company of that size, with all those resources? It made no sense. It was apparent that many of the administrative fees this insurer charged were paying for inefficiency rather than value creation.

From there, I shifted to a Fortune 100 company serving providers during the rollout of Obamacare, the largest transformation in healthcare in half a century. What actually struck me was what it *didn't* really change: providers fighting through a system they did not create, subject to a growing number of people who weren't clinicians, denied the clinical autonomy they felt they needed to serve their patients, and forced into the role of businesspeople through the incentives and guardrails created by payers.

That recognition ultimately brought me to the top of the food chain—the insurer. I joined a progressive Pennsylvania insurance company with leadership I believed in (and still do). As one of their vice presidents, I had my finger on the pulse of billions of dollars in healthcare spending. Everywhere I looked I saw a titan of business—a plan president who had risen through grit and determination, a Rhodes scholar, PhDs, and even former politicians. It was an eclectic group of beautiful minds, and it seemed they were capable of doing anything they set their collective vision on.

The company I worked for owned a hospital system—forming an "integrated delivery and financing system"—and we were up against our mirror image, a hospital system that owned an insurance company. Competition at its finest. And what did we end up doing?

Overbuilding. If we'd have been in the fuel business, you'd think we were bent on building more gas stations than there were cars. And in this case, the community paid for our ambitions through a matrix of insurance premiums and provider bills. Since both organizations were technically nonprofits, they didn't have to pay taxes of their own in exchange. Everyone was well intended. Everyone was following the rules. And where did it get us? Not to the outcomes we all desired.

Once I considered how much effort was being poured into a sector's reform, with little to show for it, I came to realize that much more was at play here. My morals and my work didn't seem to match. So I took my little "30 Under 30" trophy and set out for Silicon Valley, where I was welcomed with open arms by innovative healthcare disruptors looking, for lack of a better term, to *fuck shit up*. I was surrounded by people who weren't scared to call your baby ugly or name the very pig you were dressing with lipstick. It was a culture that thrived off antiestablishment strategies because, in our eyes, that establishment had failed to provide the affordable, high-quality service we had trusted that it would—and literally paid for.

I first joined Cricket Health, which is on a mission to revolutionize renal care, providing a value-based alternative to the many perverse and inadequate care models of today. My work there led me to Notable Health, where we built digital assistants that create clinical and administrative efficiencies via robotic process automation, simultaneously improving experiences for providers and patients alike. It was progress, in a real and meaningful way, but it still wasn't enough.

Late in 2020, I stepped back into the payer space as the CEO of Sutter Health | Aetna, one of the first ever marriages between an integrated provider network, national payer, and national retail pharmacy. It's owned jointly by Sutter Health, a twenty-four-hospital system that serves the greater Bay Area of Northern California, and Aetna, a CVS-owned national payer, which together forms the largest healthcare company in the country and the fifth-largest overall. I see it as a fascinating opportunity to align what otherwise are competing interests around the best interests of patients by taking a holistic approach to their health in what is one of the most progressive communities in the United States. I'm surrounded by people who are courageous disruptors, smarter than me, and changing the world we live in, in the midst of a local culture that not only welcomes but expects disruption. It's a great opportunity. But at best, we're a ripple, a leading indicator of change limited to fifteen California counties between the Bay Area and Sacramento.

That's why I'm writing this book and addressing it, first and foremost, to the good people in the insurance industry who are on their way up and who sense, as I did, that something's not quite right. Who have the feeling that whatever they do within their silo, it is not enough to make a real and lasting difference. Sound like you? I'm not saying your work is meaningless; rather, you may feel like you're holding a bucket and trying to save the Titanic.

My goal, in this book and in my work, is to encourage you to fuck shit up too. To give you the chutzpah to speak and think differently, to push the envelope, and to ask why—always why. I also hope that this book can help galvanize people to action, creating a forum for like-minded professionals to come together and truly change the system. And no, not at one of those conferences that are sponsored by the same entities profiting from the broken system, but rather through a transparent, open forum that is rooted in solving the issue—even if that means hurting feelings (or margins) in the process.

The need is urgent. The relentless rise in healthcare costs places a burden on employers that they can carry only by holding wages down. The rise of high-deductible plans leaves millions of insured Americans at risk of bankruptcy if they get sick, and the result of it all is a population beset by the day-to-day afflictions of chronic illness, leaving them vulnerable to catastrophe in times of pandemic.

Our currently "perfect" system is doing what it's meant to do. It's creating jobs and profits, but generating nothing like the high-quality, easily accessible, and affordable care we all desire.

I do not have all the answers. We'll have to build a better system together. It's going to take a chorus of voices, and it's a chorus that must rise from within the industry itself. The challenges are numerous and complex, but fundamental change is needed, and we're the ones to set it in motion. The government, free markets, or organizations profiting off the status quo are not going to change this industry on their own.

What gives me hope is the fact that we created this system. It's not a natural disaster. It's human-made. There's nothing to say we can't create a better one to replace it except our sense that we can't. Remember, for years, no one thought a human could run a mile in less than four minutes because no one had. But in 1954, a man named Roger Bannister—a medical student, by the way—did. And suddenly it was possible, not just for him but for others. More than 20,000 people have broken the four-minute mile since.

The race to rethink and restructure healthcare is already under way. The leading runners have completed their first lap in under a minute. Some people are going to sit and watch the race; others are going to join, thinking, *If others can do it, so can I.*

There are deep political divisions and tremendous inertia to be overcome. But we can do better, and we must. I'm simply not going to explain to my grandchildren that I knew enough to write this book but not enough to actually change things. And if you're reading this, then you're implicated now too. The time is here, before the foundation gives way and the system itself collapses.

PART 1

PERFECTLY
STUCK

CHAPTER 1

OUR (IM)PERFECT SYSTEM

I've stood in front of conferences before and made my case for a paradigm shift: our healthcare system is perfect.

"A perfect system? Ours?" I'll hear people in the audience murmuring, "He's a little bit crazy." And I can understand why they do.

For decades, critics of the US healthcare system have described it as broken, and in describing its failure, they've focused on surging prices leading to unaffordable healthcare interventions, driving further division of our socioeconomic classes, and so on. As a result, their solutions to the "broken" system begin by driving down costs, with cheerleaders for the free market on the right and more government involvement on the left.

They see systemic failures and a broken system. I see a perfect system that's failing systematically.

Why would I describe our system as perfect when I think it's failing too? Because I think we're evaluating and measuring it the wrong way. As a result, we're overlooking its core strengths. And we're not going to bring about the change we need until we recognize and agree to preserve those strengths.

POINTS OF PERFECTION

Deciding what's perfect and what's not depends on what you measure. If you choose to measure our system by the outcomes it drives—low-cost, high-quality care—then it's not perfect at all.

But what if you look at it as a jobs program that propels our economy? I'd go so far as to argue that's what it's designed to do is certainly a job it does well. We might even agree that it's money well spent—at least until it breaks the back of an American family because of the healthcare-induced debt it creates.

So what's perfect about it?

Economic growth. We have built our society on the foundation of growth driven by the healthcare sector, and we don't often recognize that. Think how hard it is to create a small company that generates enough money to pay your salary and benefits. Healthcare does that for millions of Americans, more than any other industry in our country. In most states, the single largest employer is a healthcare company (an insurance company or a hospital system). If not healthcare, it's usually Walmart. It's incredible. Where would we be without that engine?

Nobility of purpose. Experience has convinced me that the people working in healthcare, either in the direct delivery of care or the ancillary sectors that surround it, are good people. The average person working at your hospital, at the pharmaceutical company, in the insurance industry, the healthcare providers themselves—they're good people with noble, even altruistic goals. They want to have a positive impact. I'd even go so far as to say that you'll find some of the smartest, kindest people in the world working in the American healthcare system. They're not failing us; the system is failing them.

Incentives that reward. I don't want to get all Ronald Reagan here, but the fact there's so much money in American healthcare makes innovation and invention very lucrative. When you come up with a robot guided by a surgeon's hands that's more precise than the surgeon herself, or software that improves multibillion-dollar workflows, or a new blockbuster drug—name that invention—you help all of society progress. Think about it: these innovations allow us to live longer. You don't reach that type of innovative breakthrough by telling everyone they're going to be paid the same amount for their work. If you do, they'll shift their focus and effort on solving problems that have larger financial rewards. But in America, you can reap the rewards for your best ideas. That's a product of our economy, and it's not the wrong product. That is a good thing—and it would be a better thing if we captured that energy and directed it in more meaningful ways.

Longer life. Between 1800 and 2000, life expectancy in this country increased from forty years all the way to about eighty-one years now. That's exponential growth. Now, for some, living longer has meant living longer with chronic illnesses; for them, the quality of life has arguably declined. I'd rather be hit by a bus in America than anywhere else in the world, but I can't say the same for being struck by chronic disease. Still, for many, simply living long enough to see their grandchildren is a measure of the success of the system.

Ripple effects. When we think of healthcare, we think of physicians, hospitals, insurance companies, and pharmaceuticals. But the ancillary dimensions of the healthcare system—and the jobs they create—are many. There are more dialysis centers in American than there are Taco Bells, requiring daily supply chains to service them. Professors across the country teach vocational, undergraduate, and graduate students in a myriad of fields related to healthcare delivery, administration, and public health. Construction companies build profits as well as new hospitals as their local health system expands. Everywhere you look, you find the indirect benefits of healthcare's rippling economic impact.

PRESERVING WHAT'S PERFECT

When we make the mistake of talking about fixing our broken system, we tend to speak of driving costs down or of achieving greater efficiencies by stressing preventive care. Nothing wrong with efficiencies and prevention—it's exactly what an (im)perfect system needs. But if that's all we set out to do, we simply won't have the same number of jobs that we do today. I'd argue that we can't afford change at that price, not without shaking our economy to its own foundation. The effects would be devastating. It's neither plausible nor realistic, and it's certainly not desirable.

I think there is a way to preserve the jobs while creating a system that delivers higher value for the same spending. As a practical matter, that means holding the percentage of the gross domestic product devoted to healthcare at about the same level: 18 percent. As the economy grows, healthcare spending (in dollars) can grow with it. It's not a question of how much we spend but really how we spend it. And it's not a matter of eliminating jobs, because we want jobs. It's a question of what those jobs are and how to teach people—who now fill jobs created only by inefficiencies—to do the jobs we need done today in a modernized system.

There was a time when the coming of the ATM was feared because tellers would lose their jobs. And in fact, the ATM enabled banks to reduce the average number of tellers from twenty-one to thirteen in each branch. Shit! The tellers' biggest fears were coming true. But the net effect actually led to more jobs, not less, because by reducing the cost of running a branch, banks were able to open more of them. That increased access and available services. The only difference was that some of the tellers needed to learn new jobs that required new skills, which paid higher salaries as they shifted from monotonous processing to handling much more complex transactions involving wealth management and home or business financing options.

What does it all mean? That the problem isn't "fixing" the system. The problem is continuing to ensure that profits can be made and millions can be employed *while* better healthcare outcomes and experiences are achieved.

We won't find the solution to that problem by embracing the solutions offered by either the right or the left. They don't have the answers. They're why we're stuck. In the next two chapters, I'll explain why.

And hey, maybe what I'm saying is crazy. But I don't think so. By the time you're done with this book, I believe you'll agree.

CHAPTER 2

FREE MARKETS NEED NOT APPLY

"We're talking about practice. Not a game. Not the game that I go out there and die for and play every game like it's my last. Not the game. We're talking about practice, man."

—NBA STAR ALLEN IVERSON

Americans love competition, and none of us loved it more than Allen Iverson, an undersized and electrifying eleven-time all-star for the Philadelphia 76ers basketball team. He was one of the most driven stars the NBA has ever seen. And yet so complete is our obsession with competition that when he blew off practice, he got called out for it. The result was an epic Allen Iverson rant.

He knew the last thing he needed was more practice

because he was ready to play. He didn't want to be judged by the process. He wanted to be judged by the outcome.

I loved Allen Iverson.

We see competition as the answer to everything, as the single best way to drive great results. We compete in business, at school, onstage, on TV—especially TV. From *America's Got Talent* to *The Voice, Survivor, The Bachelor*, and *Shark Tank*, everything's a competition. Even cooking, an art, is a competition on TV. When COVID-19 brought a halt to sports for months, we didn't know what to do with ourselves. No sports? No competition? We thought we'd never make it.

We are wedded to the idea of winners and losers.

So it doesn't surprise me that when we talk about reforming healthcare, the go-to solution for many—particularly on the right—is competition. Transparency in prices. Consumer choice. Quality metrics. Less regulation. Unleash the free market!

Nearly all modern economists agree that the market economy *is* more productive and operates more efficiently than centrally planned economies. I agree with them. Free market economies are driven by the interplay of supply and demand, and the competition that fosters works.

But the healthcare system isn't a free market. It can't be. More competition in healthcare isn't the end-all-be-all solution for our problems. Advocates of a free-market solution have locked onto a process that can't deliver the outcomes we need. To be blunt, advocates of this approach sound just like the reporters who criticized Iverson: obsessed with a process regardless of its applicability.

PRINCIPLES OF A FREE MARKET

First, let's define the term. According to Dictionary.com, a free market is "an economic system in which prices and wages are determined by unrestricted competition between businesses, without government regulation or fear of monopolies." This being an imperfect world, there's no such thing as a perfect free market. But the guiding principles required for a successful free market are widely understood.

Elastic demand. In a free-market economy, when prices increase, demand decreases. When prices fall, demand tends to rise. That's a principle economists call elasticity. Addiction is one of just a few peculiar exceptions to the rule: when the price of heroin goes up, demand stays constant and may even increase. But that's not the case for almost everything else. Elasticity is the fuel of free-market competition.

Price transparency. In a free market, the buyer can easily understand how much something is going to cost. The price is right there on the label. It's not hidden; it's not a secret known only to some. It's easy to compare the price of one bottle of shampoo to another. Go to a restaurant, and you'll see the price of the meals before you order, not after.

Comparison of value. Price is one factor for consumers, quality another. In a free-market economy, it's easy for buyers to compare value. This car gets twenty-five miles per gallon, and another car gets eighteen. That restaurant gets three stars, this one four. This dishwasher is under warranty for one year, that one for five.

Symmetry of information. When a buyer has access to the same information about the product as the seller, that's symmetry of information. If you were to go into a Lamborghini dealership today, and the salesman said, "If you don't buy this Lamborghini today, you're going to die," you'd say, "No, I won't." Because you know that no one *needs* a Lamborghini to survive. (And so does the salesman, but that's beside the point.)

Easy entry and exit. In a free market, you want competition to come in and out of the market with as little friction as possible. If I see you open a McDonald's on one corner, I open a Burger King across the street. That leaves us competing for customers, which drives prices down. Monopolies rise when they gain an advantage that stops anyone else from taking them on.

Shoppable customer experience. If I'm in the pasta aisle at the supermarket, I can easily compare the spaghetti brands I see. They're right there next to each other with prices, ingredients, and nutrition labels, and that's what's going to drive the spaghetti I choose. I understand the entire transaction, and I'm an informed and independent consumer. Knowledge leaves me free to make an informed choice: Should I shop the pasta aisle or go find the Oreos instead? Either way, it's a consumer-driven dynamic.

HEALTHCARE LEMONADE

Now that we have some defining factors, we can ask the question: Is American healthcare capable of operating as a free market? Let's begin our analysis with a case study of a truly free market in action, then compare it with healthcare and see how they line up.

I am seven years old, and I open a lemonade stand on a hot July day. I need water, my lemonade packets, a little help from my mom, cups, and some fresh lemon slices to give my lemonade a nice look. I set up my table on the corner where two streets converge outside a popular park.

No more than two hours after I start, I'm selling lemonade at two dollars a glass. Lots of lemonade.

My neighbor Sam looks out his window, sees the line at

my stand, and decides to get in on the action. Next thing I know, he's opened his own stand across the street. He prices his lemonade at one dollar, so I drop my price too. I have to. We're in a race to the bottom—great for consumers, horrible for me.

Then Megan, my other neighbor, jumps in! Her mom didn't have any lemonade, so she's selling Kool-Aid. I can't tell if her buyers are just nice or if they prefer the Kool-Aid—but I need volume, so I drop my price to seventy-five cents to keep up the demand. I'm still in business, but it's work to hang on.

That's free-market economics, pure and simple. Level playing field, buyers driving demand, prices as transparent as a plastic glass—there's even a network effect as word spreads and families begin to come from other neighborhoods to get their choice of refreshment. Consumers get more value with prices dropping and multiple drink options available, and sellers benefit by bringing more consumers to their shops. Everyone theoretically wins.

Now let's tell the same story through a healthcare lens.

I'm still seven years old, it's still a hot July day, and I decide to sell healthcare lemonade.

First off, I have to use special lemons. They're organic, high end, the very best, grown at a special orchard. They're priced to cover all the bad lemons the farmer grew to develop his special lemons, because I have to cover his R&D costs too.

Unfortunately, I can't buy directly from the lemon farmer. I have to work through a lemon benefit manager. I'm not sure how the pricing works, but the benefits manager tells me if I buy more lemons, I can get a lemon rebate—essentially the equivalent of cash back when you use your credit card more.

Up the street, Megan is selling Kool-Aid, and I don't understand her pricing either. I barely know mine. Isn't Kool-Aid made from synthetic sugar? I wonder if consumers even realize what they're buying from her. Her quality is horrible, but then again, quality is hard to measure and even harder to market.

I've lined up my lemons. I'm ready to set up my healthcare lemonade stand.

Turns out, I need approval from the homeowners' association to put up my table. I email them, and two weeks later, I'm on the agenda. And there's Sam's mom (my competition) on the board! She has the ability to block my stand. She doesn't, but I'm guessing she's told Sam all about my plans. Why is selling lemonade, a science and an art, becoming so political?

Finally, I set up my stand. But I have to sell my lemonade in a closed container within a sealed brown paper bag. There's a lot of red tape in this healthcare lemonade business—so much that I can't tell who it's benefitting.

My neighbor Robbie, who's the first in line, can't see how much he's getting or how good it is, but the bag fee is only a dollar. Oh—and there is an additional bill I'll be sending him, because my mom, a subspecialist in this lemonade craft, is going to charge for her time too. I'm not sure how much, but I know I'll need his Social Security number, date of birth, and address so I can bill him for her efforts later.

Robbie is perplexed, but he's only on the hook for 20 percent of the cost, and he's been paying his lemonade allowance company's premiums for years without getting anything back—and dammit, he wants some lemonade. He's in.

I give Robbie the healthcare lemonade reimbursement form he'll need to fill in and send to his lemonade allowance company. But that's one complication too many, the buying experience stinks, and Robbie turns on his heel and heads across the street to Sam's stand, where things get worse.

Sam can only tell him his price compared to what he charges firefighters and police officers. It's 400 percent of his local government rack rate. Robbie doesn't even know what that means. Since Robbie can't see Sam's lemonade either, because it's in a bag too, he asks to see his reviews. Sam shows him three: five out of five, four out of five, and one out of five. *What does that mean?*

Robbie's not even sure he wants lemonade anymore. He calls the friend who referred him to my stand in the first place, a healthcare lemon broker. "Yep," the broker friend says. "You need lemonade, the government requires it, and you need to buy it at Jeb's stand."

Robbie comes back. But I'm out of lemonade at my stand, so I invite him into my living room while I get some from the kitchen. Unbeknownst to Robbie, he's now an in-buyer, not an out-buyer, and my mom—well, she paid for the furniture, so she adds a charge, which makes my bag fee higher. Same lemonade, higher fee.

Robbie glances into the kitchen, where he sees the broker friend who referred him to me in the first place, working with my mom on a fresh batch of lemonade. Now he's really pissed. "It's okay," I tell him. "He's my business partner, and I pay him a salary. It's not like he's getting a kickback on your cup of lemonade."

Complicated enough for you? Does that sound much like a "free market"? The sad fact is that's only about 25 percent of the bullshit involved in the world of healthcare lemonade.

The dynamics that a truly free market requires are nowhere in sight. You have a supplier competing in an unfair market. You have a buyer who doesn't know the price, how much he'll owe, how much he's getting, its quality, or if he even needs it. He's also got a person he trusts telling him he has to buy it, even though that person has an undisclosed financial interest.

The only player in the market who can see the big picture is the lemonade allowance company, for which Robbie's employer foots the majority of the bill. It's their business to follow the money from the lemon farmer to my stand to Robbie's wallet—oh, and don't forget that random bill my mom will send for sitting inside our house on her furniture. As you can see, they're in a unique position to help.

But you know what? This system might just be too sweet for them to change.

"FREEING" THE HEALTHCARE MARKET

Let's walk through the guiding principles of a free-market economy to see how many apply to healthcare.

Elastic demand: No. If I find out that my fiancée is bleeding from the brain and needs an MRI, she's getting an MRI. It doesn't matter what the cost is when it's a question of life and death. I don't care if I need to sell the car, sell the house—she's getting an MRI. The same is true of chronic illness. Diabetics need insulin to survive. The demand is inelastic.

Price transparency: No. In healthcare, your billed rate changes based on your insurance, your copay, your coinsurance, whether you're in network or out of network, and so on. Hospitals can base their rates off a chargemaster; the deal your insurance company struck with the hospital determines the discount you get off the master price. Patients may be classified by diagnosis-related group (DRG), a cost-containment measure that standardizes the payment the hospital receives for treating everyone with your categorized condition. Oh, and did you switch from a PPO to an HMO last year, or maybe your spouse did? What's your discount on the hospital menu price? What's the cost of the fries in your healthcare value meal? The patient doesn't know, at least not until after they've "eaten" it—and the doctor who's cooking usually doesn't either.

Comparison of value: No. We'd all agree that not every doctor is created equal. But we have a very difficult time objectively measuring and differentiating providers based on outcomes. There are too many variables, and too many of them are unquantifiable. That's why marketing for healthcare companies is more a branding exercise than anything else. We ascribe higher quality to bigger brands—but size doesn't necessarily correlate to high-quality outcomes.

Symmetry of information: No. Doctors talk to patients in what amounts to a second language that patients can't understand. If a doctor says, "Jeb, you need an MRI; you're bleeding from the brain right now," I don't know whether he's right. I don't know if I'm bleeding from the brain; I don't know if I need an MRI or a CT scan; I don't know if I need to be talking to a neurosurgeon or a radiologist. I don't know. I can't know. And second opinions usually just make it more confusing, not less.

Easy entry and exit: No. How hard is it to build a hospital? Open a surgery center? Think about how many years a physician goes to school before they can even open a practice. Healthcare is less a world of easy access to the market than it is a world of market allocation, where competitors effectively define their turf and others stay off. About a dozen states require a Certificate of Need (CON) review, a contentious regulatory wrestle that governs the building of healthcare facilities. The purpose is preventing the creation of excess capacity that leads to higher rates, but some say the effect is fostering minimonopolies in the name of protecting consumers.

Shoppable customer experience: No. How many things in healthcare are truly shoppable? When's the last time you compared drug prices at three different pharmacies? MRI charges for inpatient facilities versus ambulatory outpatient services? And if it's an acute situation, no shopping is possible. If you're in a hospital after a car crash and you need a chest X-ray, you're not asking to go somewhere else to get it or compare and then coming back. For the vast majority of Americans, healthcare simply isn't a shoppable experience.

CONSUMERISM

Far from being a free market, the healthcare system is so convoluted and entangled that consumers don't actually exist, at least in the economic sense of the term. The vast majority of transactions in healthcare are simply not shoppable experiences; there's no fair and equitable marketplace where buyers and sellers can conduct their business.

But that hasn't stopped free-market reformers from pushing for "consumerism" in healthcare. That's the term they use and the goal they seek. Are they right? Is that what we're after?

Let's start again with a definition. Merriam-Webster defines *consumerism* as "the theory that an increasing consumption of goods is economically desirable." Is consuming more healthcare our individual goal or the system's goal? For me, as an individual, it's the opposite, because the more healthcare I consume, the sicker I must be and inevitably the more I spend—to the point of wiping out my savings and potentially losing my home.

Here's another definition from Dictionary.com: consumerism is "the concept that an ever-expanding consumption of goods is advantageous to the economy." Well, yes, the healthcare system is set up to drive our economy. That's what makes it (im)perfect. But our goal in reforming healthcare isn't increasing the amount of healthcare we consume. It's achieving higher-quality care, better personal health, and an affordable price for all.

When we talk about consumerism, we're on the wrong subject using the wrong language.

CHOICE

You want another nail in the competition coffin?

When it comes to lemonade stands, you can go to another street. You have your choice of grocery stores and restaurants, gas stations and car dealerships.

But in healthcare, you have no choice. That's because someone else is usually making the choices for you.

Consider the choice architecture built into health insurance. Go for a preventive checkup, and there's no deductible; see your primary care doc for a standard appointment, and it's twenty dollars; see a specialist, and your deductible jumps to one hundred dollars. Insurance product architecture involves the introduction of various levels of financial friction intended to guide your behavior.

I'm not making a case against nudging people toward good healthcare decisions. The point I'm trying to make is that we're nudging them *by taking away* the choice they think they have—the choice a free-market system requires. I've actually counted and believe that roughly seventy-five choices are made for the employee before the employee is given their opportunity to weigh in. Think about it! The employer decides which broker to use, when to go out to bid for a new insurance quote, what requirements are set by the employer, contribution amounts from the employee, the network of providers, the buy-ups, the wellness programs; we're talking something like 98 percent baked before it comes to the employee.

It's the equivalent of the parents' gambit at mealtime with their toddler: Would you like an apple or a banana? In reality, the parents have already made the choice. They went to the grocery store and picked out the fruit. They considered what kind of snack the child should have. By the time they put the apple and the banana in front of their toddler, the big choices have already been made.

That's exactly what an employer does when picking an insurance company and the product menu they offer their employees. Apple or banana? Sam's lemonade or Megan's

Kool-Aid? Never mind the fact that the employer might be guided by a "consultant" who is paid more by Sam than Megan to refer their drinks. Gee, I wonder how that will turn out!

That may look like a free market, but it isn't. Thank goodness we're only talking about apples and bananas, lemonade or Kool-Aid. Can you imagine how we'd feel if someone's very life or death depended on this model?

So if the right is misguided in its insistence on a free-market solution to our healthcare woes, does that mean the left has a better answer in a government-driven solution? I don't think so. Let's talk about why.

CHAPTER 3

DR. GOVERNMENT WILL SEE YOU NOW...

"If you can't convince them, confuse them."

—PRESIDENT HARRY S. TRUMAN DESCRIBING
HIS OPPONENTS' TACTICS

For almost one hundred years, the citizens of the United States have allowed the government to influence the healthcare industry and the delivery of care. The result is one of the most convoluted systems in the world, with some of the most expensive interventions and lowest quality outcomes among comparable countries. We've allowed healthcare, which is a science and an art, to become completely politicized. If you think that's a good thing, pause and consider our country's response to a global pandemic.

Remember when we were all voting for the president of the United States and we didn't need an exit poll to tell who was voting for whom because whether they were wearing a mask served as a proxy? Yeah, me neither.

I do believe the government has a role to play in healthcare, and it's a vital one. As I hope I made clear in the last chapter, the free market, competition-solves-all solutions favored by many is not the answer.

But neither are the bigger government solutions favored by many of our friends on the left.

Let me unfold my thinking first by stating two things that I believe are givens.

Whether you come down on the right or the left, I believe we should all be able to agree on this: the politicization of healthcare isn't serving us well. It's left us paralyzed. We opened the last decade by passing Obamacare in March of 2010 and spent the rest of it absorbed in fights over undoing it.

We should be able to agree on this too: our government has demonstrated again and again that it shouldn't be involved directly in clinical care. It can set guardrails and provide financial assistance, but direct clinical care from the government is a line like the TSA's: I don't want to be in it.

Consider the Veterans Health Administration hospital scandal of 2014, when workers falsified their waitlist because they couldn't meet their obligations to veterans in need of care. Patients died while waiting for appointments.

In 2020, COVID-19 caught the government completely unprepared, leading to a mad scramble for PPE and ventilators needed to protect healthcare workers and save the critically ill. The Trump administration's small-government slant left pandemic management decisions to the states, and as a result, we had science being interpreted ten or fifteen or fifty different ways. (It was hard to keep up.)

I'm not trying to be political here. But if we can't get a pandemic response right, how the hell are we going to pull off Medicare for All?

There's this too: think about your recent customer service experiences with the IRS, the DMV, the TSA. Compare those to your recent user experiences with Amazon, Netflix, Lyft, and Venmo. Choose any government agency you want and compare it to the private sector. When it comes to healthcare—a matter of life and death—do we want the creative and innovative energy of the government or the private sector driving us forward?

HOW WE GOT HERE

Before I discuss the essential role that I do see government playing, I think it's helpful to take a walk down history lane, reviewing the steps that got us here.

Modern-day health insurance was born in Texas in 1929 with the formation of the first Blue Cross health plan. The plan arose out of the efforts by administrators at the Baylor University Hospital trying to find a way to make hospital care more affordable for its patients, many of whom were public school teachers in Dallas. The cost was fifty cents a month, and the plan was a form of prepayment for up to twenty-one days of hospital care. The plan was an immediate success, and soon, administrators were enrolling workers in other professions across the city. Blue Shield evolved in a similar way for physicians and medical groups, and the two companies began to come together in the 1940s.

The Great Depression and massive unemployment that swept the country in the 1930s led to the creation of the welfare state and its safety net, embodied in the Social Security program. From the first, the program depended on today's workers to support retirees; the money they pay in goes right back out. The first Social Security check was issued on January 31, 1940, to Ida May Fuller, who retired at sixty-five. A legal secretary, Ida May paid a total of $24.75 in Social Security taxes; her first check of $22.54 nearly offset her contribution. She lived to one hundred and collected a total of nearly $23,000 in benefits.

I add Ida May's details because people love to showcase Social Security as the epitome of what government programs can do. It's not the government at work here; it's just math. The system worked for Ida because at the outset, we had 150 people working and paying taxes into the system for every single Social Security beneficiary on the other end of the equation. We've barely modified the system since, people are living longer, and now we're at three people working for every Social Security beneficiary.

It's a lot like healthcare. With the government underpaying (based on the current state of efficiency in care delivery) for services it delivers through Medicare, what happens when commercial lines of business can no longer keep rising because employers and employees have buckled under the weight of cross-subsidizing the feds? What happens when the percentage of people over sixty-five climbs from 15 to 20 percent? We're on track to do just that in the next few decades. When math stops being math and becomes politics, it doesn't work.

The country came to a fork in the road on healthcare following World War II and arguably took the wrong path. As millions of soldiers came home from war, the government capped wages in order to control inflation. That left businesses to find other ways to compete for talent. One of the benefits they created to attract workers was employer-sponsored health insurance, which remains today the single most common form of health coverage. The result was inequity: the employed population had access to insurance, and those who were disabled or unemployed did not. Other developed countries did not follow suit. At about this time, for example, Canada opted for its single-payer system.

The pressure to address that issue gave rise to Medicare and Medicaid, passed into law in 1965 through a massive push by President Johnson, a master of political dealmaking. Medicare, which provided health coverage for the elderly, and Medicaid, providing it for the poor, were initially far more limited than they are today. Together with CHIP, which provides coverage for children in need, they are administered by the Centers for Medicare and Medicaid Services (CMS) and provide coverage to more than 100 million Americans. That makes the government the single largest insurer in the country—and the single largest buyer of healthcare as measured by covered lives. Boy, why does that remind me of Fannie Mae and Freddie Mac?

Perhaps not surprisingly, we've been fighting over the government's role in health insurance ever since these programs were created. In the 1980s, Republican Ronald Reagan made his case against big government with quips like this: "The nine most terrifying words in the English language are, 'I'm from the government and I'm here to help.' " On the other side of the aisle, Democrats pushed for more, not less. Clintoncare, an ambitious reimagining of American healthcare, fell flat, though he still delivered CHIP. Barack Obama made expanding healthcare access a priority and won passage of the Patient Protection and Affordable Care Act in 2010. Of course, no one calls it the PPACA; it's Obamacare. What could be a better indication of the politicization of American healthcare than that?

So here we stand today, where our views on healthcare are determined by our political outlook. We've moved completely away from a standard of care based on facts grounded in science and math. Instead, we're playing a game of political ping-pong, left versus right, and it shows no sign of ending.

Where has this gotten us?

The Organization for Economic Co-Operation and Development (OECD) is an international organization that tracks both the cost and quality of healthcare across comparable nations. When it comes to cost, we're number one, with the highest cost per capita. When it comes to quality? Fifteenth. We've created the most expensive system in the world, and we're producing some of the poorest outcomes. The government's role in healthcare has become so large that it has incredible implications on the entire market, and it's hard to argue that the results are good.

Again, this is not to say that I don't see a role for government in healthcare or that everything it's touched has gone wrong. In fact, there's one program—Medicare Advantage—that may show us a way forward. Advantage is built on the chassis of Medicare, which is a "big government" program. But it's essentially a *privatized* form of Medicare, leaving local organizations to run the program on behalf of the government. Those local organizations are given a financial incentive—profits—to deliver high-quality care at the lowest possible cost. To prevent those organizations from reaming the American public, they must meet quality standards, and their margins are capped at about 15 percent. That means 85 percent of the dollars need to be spent on healthcare and quality improvement activities, and the results are promising.

GOVERNING PRINCIPLES

In Chapter 2, I outlined the guiding principles for a successful free market and showed the many ways in which they just don't apply to healthcare. I'll do the same here, by listing the guiding principles that would characterize a successful big-government approach to healthcare.

Self-sustaining programs free of private sector cross-subsidies: No. Quite the opposite! CMS and the programs it administers have demonstrated a limited capability in sustainably controlling cost. Medicare, Medicaid, and

CHIP are structured in ways that give the people they cover no incentive to keep costs down. Numerous studies have shown that when people face no financial barriers to care—zero coinsurance, no deductible—utilization, especially in avoidable high-cost settings of care, skyrockets in the wrong direction. It's a delicate balance, because these are programs designed to serve those in need, but experiments have shown things as modest as a five-dollar copay will negatively influence a patient seeking care.

Rather than work to influence the behavior of Medicaid and Medicare recipients, the government has controlled costs by artificially slowing the increase of unit cost—that is, by controlling and subduing the reimbursement rate providers are paid. That leaves providers no choice but to treat their commercial line of business as their source of profits. How do they gain the weight needed to negotiate better rates with commercial insurance companies? By building healthcare conglomerates to gain as much market share as possible.

If you're going to go down the government path on healthcare, you can't be half pregnant. You're either all in or all out. Private industry is keeping our government programs afloat, and not just with our taxes but through financial support to providers via higher commercial reimbursement rates paid largely by the employer.

Political consensus: No. A *hard* no. There's a large divide in this country around the core philosophical question of whether healthcare is a right or a privilege. It remains an open question.

The ACA gave states incentives to expand Medicaid coverage to the poor, and most conservative states said no. In the years that followed, as the economy surged, it wasn't a problem. But with the pandemic, millions of Americans lost their jobs, and with it their insurance, shining a new light on that decision. Do we really want to say healthcare is a privilege or change the eligibility so drastically by state when unavoidable hard times leave millions at risk?

Even if you take the position that it is a privilege, the math says that paying for proactive, preventive care makes "cents." Take hypertension (HTN) for example—high blood pressure. It's treated easily and cheaply with beta blockers that cost, at the high end, about a hundred dollars per year per patient. What are the possible consequences of untreated HTN? A heart attack or stroke. The cost of treating either comes in somewhere between $6,000 and $12,000, and that's without me including high-priced "outliers" that would really embarrass some of my industry friends. That's enough money to buy between sixty and a hundred years of beta blockers. We're all going to pay the bill for uncompensated care received by others, either through higher taxes or increased rates at the local hospital. I'd rather keep someone healthy, simply because it's the right thing to do and it saves money!

Do you see how a democratic ideology (government-sponsored preventive care) can provide the fiscally conservative (avoided costly heart attack) and morally correct desirable outcome? If it's a math problem and not a political choice, the correct answer is clear—but we can't seem to get there. What's blocking us? A lack of faith, for one thing; people don't trust the government to be involved in their healthcare decisions. An imbalance of argument, for another. Most of the research and articles framing the debate on healthcare come from university-based academics who tend to be liberal in outlook. And they're making their voices heard through their publications and the students they influence.

Positive or neutral impact on economy: No. Healthcare is the largest employer in the country, and the government insures more Americans through Medicare, Medicaid, and CHIP than any health insurance company. Government decisions have the potential to rock the economy in a negative way. It's also been reported that the government—meaning taxpayers—is covering hundreds of billions in unnecessary spending attributable to waste, fraud, and abuse.

Long-term focus for success: No. Politicians live in two-to four-year life cycles. Promising programs like population health management—focused on social inputs like housing, labor, and education that affect health—take five to ten years to even gain a foothold. The math works; these are wise investments. But the politics don't. Not in our environment. We're ten years in on Obamacare and still debating what works and what doesn't, what needs to be reformed or rejected or not. The incentives of the people governing these programs are not aligned with the outputs of the programs themselves.

Freedom from external influences: No! A total of $450 million to $600 million is spent on healthcare and pharmaceutical lobbying every year. That is the amount that's publicly reported and easily tracked, not piped through some random PAC with a cryptic name. It far outweighs almost any other industry—all in an effort to sway the political forces that govern your healthcare coverage. Remember, one in every three Americans has government-sponsored healthcare coverage. The healthcare sector as a whole accounts for one in every five dollars spent in America. We've placed large decisions in the hands of a small group of people, many of them career politicians, who are subject to money-is-no-limit lobbying efforts. It's scary to think of that dynamic's influence on science-based matters of life and death.

It's not just a question of what's going on in Washington

either. In my hometown of Wilmington, Delaware, we've seen a person with twenty years of police experience and a handful of years as sheriff run for and win the position of state insurance commissioner. I don't want to put this guy on blast; he's a nice man. But the fact is that the man responsible for the insurance practices in the state of Delaware doesn't have enough experience in the field to qualify for most entry-level roles in an insurance company. That should signal something.

IT'S NOT POLITICAL

Government's extensive involvement in American healthcare has made what should be mathematical and scientific into a matter of opinion. As our politics have grown more polarized, we've made healthcare policy a matter of ideology instead of science. Worse yet, it's said that fake news spreads six times faster than real news due to social media and the algorithms that govern what you see. Said differently, we're less objectively informed when making our voting decisions. Left and right have locked their horns. At a time when we need to be talking in creative, open-minded views of the appropriate role for government in a reimagined healthcare system, we're in a shouting match that's not going anywhere.

But neither are the pressures that threaten to bring the system we're living with down. The insurance companies that are feeling that pressure from the employers who pay the bills have tried a series of self-reforms in response. Those unfortunately haven't worked either, and we'll look at why next.

PART 2

THE FAILURE OF SELF-REFORM

CHAPTER 4

LOOKING FOR VALUE IN VALUE-BASED REIMBURSEMENT

"It is difficult to get a man to understand something when his salary depends upon his not understanding it."

—UPTON SINCLAIR

Health insurance companies haven't argued against the need for change in the industry. Ask industry leaders and they'll agree: the health outcomes are not where they should be. The quality is not where it should be. The user experience is not where it should be. Regulation is not where it should be. Given all these shortcomings, you'd at least think healthcare would be affordable. But the cost is not where it should be either.

As the price for these unsatisfactory results rose, pressure from the federal government and employers who were paying the majority of the insurance bill for their beneficiaries and employees rose with it. Something had to be done. And payers focused their initial efforts to self-reform on an obvious problem over which they had complete control: financial incentives.

Of the trillions of dollars spent in this country on medical care and pharmaceuticals, almost all of it is tied to the service being rendered or the product consumed. Not the necessity of the product or service, not its outcome—and not even avoiding the underlying healthcare issue altogether.

Insurance companies and CMS set out to turn that dynamic upside down by rewriting the incentives defined in the reimbursement contracts they negotiate with healthcare providers. Instead of paying for the service, they'd pay for the outcome, rewarding the processes that produced better results. It's not a new idea; its roots can be traced to the sixties and seventies. But it didn't step into the spotlight until 2010, with the passage of Obamacare.

It sounds great. Shit, I bought into it; I won my "30 Under 30" award in Pittsburgh for helping to create Value-Based Reimbursement (VBR) programs and roll them into the local provider market.

There are a lot of people out there who say that VBR has cracked the nut, that it's bent the curve, and for evidence, they point to the fact that when measured as a percentage of GDP, healthcare spending remained static over the past decade. It has looked good, but that's misleading. Until the pandemic struck, economic growth had been surging. VBR didn't actually bend the curve of healthcare spending as much as some would say—because that spending was simply racing alongside a fast-moving economy.

Broadly speaking, VBR programs simply haven't lived up to their potential. And they won't, not until they are integrated into a fundamentally new approach to healthcare in this country.

DEFINITIONS, GOALS, AND REALITY

Let's begin, as always, by defining our terms in my layman's language.

In the dominant **Fee for Service** (FFS) payment model, services are unbundled and paid for separately. Your visit to the ER, your X-ray, your CT scan, your surgery, your overnight hospital stay, your visit with the physical therapist—all of it.

There are a few varieties of FFS that blur these lines, such as case rates or Diagnosis-Related Groups (DRG) for inpatient utilization, which amount to a bundled FFS paid as a flat rate per diem. (Anyone who is deep into the reimbursement game understands how health systems can bury massive differences in facility and professional fees.)

There are plenty of textbooks on reimbursement methodologies, so I'll spare you the details. But broadly speaking, providers continue to be financially incentivized to provide sick care, not healthcare.

In practice, this gives physicians an incentive to provide more treatments and order more tests because payment is largely dependent on the quantity of care rather than the quality of care. The compensation received by many employed providers is based on RVUs—**Relative Value Units**—which are essentially a measure of the relative value the provider creates for the organization that employs them. Do more surgeries, order more labs, touch more patients, and you'll accrue more RVUs.

Of course, no one will put it like that. Instead, RVUs are commonly portrayed as a methodology the CMS put forth to ensure physician skill, site of care, patient acuity, and volume of services, which were all factored into a metric that could assist with correctly compensating providers.

That was in fact CMS's intention. It's a legitimate methodology. But like many things in healthcare, this has played out in what is a classic scenario: CMS introduces a reform, and then private industry bastardizes the constructs, intentions, and mechanics to meet their needs. It sounds like the industry is applying CMS logic—but only until you look at what they're actually tracking: the percentage of value each provider creates for them. In practice, RVUs have been twisted to become one more way to guide providers to get paid more by doing more.

Value-Based Reimbursement (VBR) is the alternative compensation model. Under this approach, instead of rewarding providers for the number of services they perform, incentives are structured to reward them for better clinical and financial outcomes—higher quality of care, greater affordability. Instead of rewarding overutilization, VBR seeks to reward avoiding or delaying disease progression by closing gaps in care and heading off the higher costs inherent in acute situations. If the patient is a diabetic, VBR would reward the provider for ensuring the patient gets their annual influenza vaccination, urine examination for proteinuria, aspirin prescription, and so on; better yet, VBR would reward the provider when the patient successfully keeps their hemoglobin A1c in check.

VBR principles are embedded at the heart of Obamacare and have been popularized by the Institute for Healthcare Improvement (IHI) around the "triple aim:"

- Improving the individual experience of care

- Improving the health of populations
- Reducing the per capita costs of care for populations

A fourth pillar—provider experience—has emerged over the past several years, as research focused attention on the emerging problems of wellness and burnout among providers who complained of the growing burdens of technology and administrative tasks. This has been supported as the country continues to grapple with clinician shortages. (I'll respond to this problem in Part 3.)

Beginning a decade ago, CMS has been guided by this multipronged mission statement, and insurance companies have chased the same goals. It's been a massive wave of effort, sweeping through the public and private sectors. Theoretically, it makes complete sense.

Yet very little has changed.

Today, despite a commitment to VBR principles at the top, the vast majority of employed providers continue to be paid on an FFS/RVU basis: the more they do, the more they make. Why? There are a number of reasons, but the biggest is this: VBR is stuck at the cost centers of provider organizations, the nitty-gritty dynamics involving compensation. A general rule of organizational behavior—which no one wants to change—becomes all the more true when the change involves how they're paid.

It's not as if the drivers of change didn't anticipate resistance. They created what's often called a "glide path," intended to lead provider organizations from the shallow end to the deep end of the VBR swimming pool. At the shallow end, rewards for rudimentary performance programs, for the processes necessary to yield success. Think of this as being rewarded for the "blocking and tackling" of value-based mechanics—providers are incentivized to lay the foundation for success. In a few years, the deep end: shared accountability for patient outcomes and costs. Deliver the desired outcome at low costs, and the provider wins; fall short, and the provider's margin dwindles. In the most aggressive VBR programs, a provider who falls far enough might even end up owing money back to the insurer.

What's the result? Providers are getting stuck at the shallow end of the pool. The deeper in the pool they get, the more risk they take on and the harder it becomes to make the margins they were making before. A lot of provider organizations are backed by private equity companies or private investors; some are even for-profit and publicly traded. They are growth stocks, not value stocks, and they need to make money.

Worse yet, these glide paths can actually hurt providers. Imagine this scenario: a provider is running their horribly inefficient practice at two times the Risk-Adjusted Market Average (as a close friend eloquently named it, "RAMA")—

meaning their costs are twice that of other providers with a similar patient mix. The provider is introduced to VBR and told over the next three to five years, they are going to be transitioned from an FFS model onto a capitated rate, which is a fixed reimbursement rate per head. Guided from the shallow end to the deep end of the pool. So, acting on what they're shown, they begin to slowly but surely pull inefficiencies out of their cost structure, eventually getting to year five, when they're hypothetically as close to efficient as possible. And *boom!* They're given a capitated rate that is a few points higher than their current cost. Wait! What? Any provider who sees that coming will dig in their heels; far better for them to have taken the capitated rate in year one, while most of their inefficiencies were still built into their rate—and thus, their future profit margin.

My scenario is overly simplistic, but the dynamics I'm describing are real. Don't get me wrong. I'm all for squeezing inefficiency out of delivery systems. I'm not arguing right or wrong here; I'm just describing reality. As they go down the glide-path route, providers gain confidence in managing financial risk—but they also give away precious margin. Even if that margin is based on an inflated baseline to begin with. They will resist that.

Think of it this way: imagine if your boss came to you and said, "Hey, we know we're paying you a salary now, and you've got kids in college and a mortgage and all that. But...

here's the thing. Over the next two or three years, we're going to shift somewhere between 10 and 50 percent of your salary into more of a variable comp—based on how you interact with others, the outcomes of the meetings you're in, how fast you respond to emails. That sort of thing."

How would you feel? What if your spouse, who has a job similar to yours, got the same talk on the same day at her company, but all their metrics were different?

You'd dig in your heels too. You wouldn't want to be compensated based on things you can't control, or things that other employees can negatively affect—especially if your boss can't entirely explain how to achieve them or even report on them in a timely fashion. Meanwhile, you're asked to make this switch because the company's cost has gotten too high—but wait. Are your compensation and inherent incentives really the driver of that issue?

Can you imagine if a manager had this talk with you, while the company has increased the number of people managers five times over the past two decades? And yet you, the worker, are still the issue?

What we've seen is that providers are okay with what's called "performance risk"—compensation based on managing the processes, interactions, and general outcomes of the diabetic sitting in their waiting room. Something they can control. It's another proposition altogether to hold them accountable for what we call "actuarial risk"—that is risk that is far outside their control and can swing heavily if they don't have an adequately sized panel of attributed patients.

STRUCTURAL ISSUES

VBR is a bright, shiny object that everyone theoretically agrees with. Let's look more closely at why it begins to fall apart when you put it into action.

PROGRAM CONSENSUS

Every single insurance carrier has instituted a value-based program, if not multiple VBR programs. It might be for primary care, it might be for specialists, it might be for hospitals, but they have all developed these programs.

And they're all different. They have very different quality metrics. They have different methodologies for measuring success. Their VBR and FFS payment mix varies. A provider organization may have anywhere from a handful to more than fifteen health plans represented across their overall patient panel. It's very, very difficult for the provider to manage all these programs. We're not making their life any simpler at all, but the opposite. I certainly applaud the trade organizations that proclaimed a need for consensus on programs—I mean it seems fairly simple and logical that consistency would behoove everyone.

Given the hand they've been dealt, providers are either going to focus on the programs that serve the largest portion of their patient panel or on the metrics that are most common across multiple programs, while skipping the idiosyncratic ones. So if you're an insurer and don't have a material market share, good luck influencing that provider with your value-based program; they're simply not going to have the bandwidth or resources to pay attention to it. If your market share is in the 25 to 50 percent range, it's a different story; you can compel the provider to make a change—or at least try. Push too hard, and there's always the risk the provider will push back and threaten, "Sorry, we're not going to accept your coverage anymore." If they've got the size or "share of care" to take that stand, the insurer loses precious network access, which can directly impact membership sales and retention.

Force providers into the deep end of the pool, and they will rise up against you.

BEHAVIORAL ECONOMICS

The goal in changing incentives is to change behavior in the face of resistance. But typically, VBR still represents only 5 to 10 percent of a provider's total reimbursement. The rest is still FFS.

That's like giving a child an allowance of one hundred dollars a month, then throwing in an extra five dollars if the child does their chores really well, and an extra five dollars on top of that if you never have to remind them to take out the trash. The incentive is such a small percentage of the total that most kids would say, "Screw it! I've already got a hundred bucks. Why do that too?"

You'll hear insurers proclaim over 90 percent of their payments are covered by value-based programs. This is the math equivalent of putting lipstick on a pig. It's creative accounting, not reality.

Here's how it works. The carrier will put as many primary care docs as it can on a VBR program. They're the smallest fish in the pond, directly responsible for just 5 percent of the total cost of care. But under VBR, the total cost of care those patients receive—meaning the other 95 percent, beyond the PCP's control!—is attributed to those PCPs. Hence the carrier's metric (and their claim) that the vast majority of their payments are covered by their VBR program. The reality? That 95 percent of costs can actually be paid on an FFS basis.

That's not driving meaningful change. That's playing make-believe for marketing's sake. VBR programs can't deliver results until the big fish—the hospital systems—are incentivized in the same way the PCPs are. But the big fish are making out pretty well in the current state of affairs, thank you very much, and for that matter, the carriers are too.

There's a second problem with VBR incentives. You remember Pavlov's dogs, right? Ring a bell, give the dog a treat; after just a few repetitions, Pavlov found the dogs began to salivate as soon as they heard the bell. They could taste the treat even before they got it.

Most VBR programs are based on claims. Let's say the provider does what they're incentivized to do—they talk to the diabetic who hasn't had a foot exam in three years about the importance of making an appointment, and they actually get the patient to come in and close a critical gap in care. It's captured within the claim they submit to their insurer. The provider has to successfully submit the claim, the insurer needs to process the claim, and then the insurer needs to ensure enough time for "run out" and then analyze a large swath of claims. Somewhere from three and eighteen months later, the provider gets paid for their behavior.

And there's a kicker. Progressive VBR programs use percentiles within a market to provide protection for market changes beyond any one provider's control.

Example: VBR programs often reward providers for reducing avoidable, high-cost emergency services incurred by their patients. Well, when COVID-19 became a national pandemic, emergency department utilization dropped because people who might have gone to the emergency department (ED) didn't for fear they'd catch the virus there. It wasn't because of anything providers did. So VBR programs are structured to reward only the top percentile of providers in a given market, the ones who truly outperform the market norm. It takes time for the insurer to figure that out and even longer to report on and consequently reward.

FFS payments are much more closely tied; when the provider drops the claim, they know they're getting paid for the service. There may be the occasional denial or need for additional information, but their behavior is tied closely to a positive financial incentive.

With FFS, Pavlov's dog is salivating. With VBR, not so much.

FAULTY PROGRAMS

In practice, VBR programs have proven very difficult to administer. Measurement methodologies are one of the hot-button issues to consider. A classic example is measuring pediatricians on vaccination rates. What if they serve a community with a disproportionate amount of antivaxxers? Are you going to penalize a provider for following the wishes of the parents? Patient attribution is another challenge. Every patient's outcome needs to be tied to a particular provider. But what if you're a PCP in the cold north whose attributed patient heads to Florida for two months every winter, where they see an unmanaged doctor who orders all sorts of exams? Is the PCP in the north accountable for the costs that the Florida doctor runs up? The answer is often yes. Why? Because the insurer that is also based in and serving the cold north is most likely directly or indirectly financially liable.

Reporting lag is another challenge. Reports are often based on claims and generated by the insurance carrier, and I've already talked about the lag between dropping a claim at one end and getting a report out the other. Compounding the delay is the fact that providers don't drop claims the same day they see you; in the case of CMS patients, the provider can take up to six months. The consequence? Say a patient is a hypochondriac, an emergency room frequent flyer. If the provider doesn't know that the patient is attributed to them, doesn't know the patient is frequenting the ED, and doesn't know why the patient is utilizing the ED, then what are they supposed to do?

It's as if you're a head coach in the NBA finals, and it's time to call the final play with the game on the line. But the only data you've got comes from the first two quarters of the game. You don't know if someone's gotten hurt. You don't know who's shooting well. You've got to make a big-time decision with very limited insight. It's most likely not going to end well.

The holy grail of most of these programs is a metric called "Total Cost of Care." The metric is quite interesting; it's an effort to make a single provider responsible for the total cost of care a patient incurs. That means everything from their hospital visits to their prescriptions to their primary and specialty care. It makes sense in theory; I'd want a single provider to give a shit about everything I'm doing related to my health.

But no provider can manage the unit cost of each service a patient receives. That's negotiated by the insurance carrier. A provider can manage part of the cost equation—utilization—but not the negotiated cost of the service itself. If the provider lives in a community with a large health system that has the muscle to negotiate high unit-cost rates, and the patient goes to that hospital instead of a smaller, lower-cost hospital elsewhere in the community—well, too bad for the provider.

No carrier would ever admit to structuring a program with the purpose of generating tension between health systems and small independent providers, but the fact is that they benefit when that's the case. The last thing they want is to drive small providers to the cover of working for the big system.

What would that mean for the insurer? Well, the health system that negotiates with them for reimbursement just got that much stronger, controlling that much more of the clinician base and therefore attributable patient population. Next time you go to them to negotiate rates, they've got even more weight to throw around. What's more, the health system is going to use its PCPs to drive referrals to its specialists and its labs and its imaging centers—and guess what, that's right, those sites of service may have a hefty facility fee associated with it. Not every integrated system does it purely for the money. Unfortunately, this tactic is often engulfed in the argument that we need more coordinated care, which is easier to do in a closed system where all providers are employed by the same entity. There's truth to that, but it's true that this serves as a convenient excuse for the facilities that are profiteering off this referral play. Just look for the data indicating that their cost and utilization is less than a loosely affiliated group of providers.

Encouraging tension between providers and health systems is not a stated strategy of insurance companies, and I'm not even saying it's a deliberate goal—but it sure is an interesting dynamic to ponder.

Finally, there's another contentious element to the foundation on which VBR programs sit: stop loss. That's the threshold (or "attachment point") set to acknowledge the very expensive cases that are beyond any provider's control—a traumatic accident, metastasizing cancer whose cause is unknown, end-stage renal disease. The challenge for the provider is that insurers set different eligibility criteria and absolute stop-loss thresholds over which the providers have no control. In one case, it might be $100,000; in another, $250,000. That means a provider could be on the hook for one patient who cost $150,000 with one insurer but not another. Very confusing!

All of this amounts to extra burdens we're asking providers to manage on top of doing the one thing they were actually trained to do: practice medicine.

CUMBERSOME OPERATIONS

The fact is that most insurers don't have the ability to provide the administrative support needed to make a VBR machine hum. The machine looks great, but once you put it in motion, it's clunky.

A great example is a payment model called a "prospective bundle." Consider a total hip replacement. We can all agree on the standard of care: there's pre-op work, the surgery itself, post-op follow-up, and some rehab. We might agree on the math too. Add all these things up, and the episode of care cost is about $45,000.

Under a prospective-bundle VBR program, the predominant billing provider (the orthopedic surgeon) is paid $45,000 up front, at the beginning of the episode of care.

That's intended to create an incentive for the provider to reduce avoidable costs while maintaining or increasing the quality of care. And if the actual cost goes above $45,000, the provider is liable for the difference.

Sounds terrific—until you encounter the operational challenges. The claim for each of the components needs to be zeroed out in the insurer's claim adjudication and accounting system because the surgeon's been prepaid. To compound the confusion, imagine a patient on a self-funded employer insurance plan—an **Administrative Services Only** (ASO) program, using the carrier largely to provide a network of providers and process claims. Perhaps the employer doesn't want to support these incentives and believes that they should only pay the provider's cost. And what happens if that patient's primary care provider is managing a total-cost-of-care metric? How do you accrue against that?

Finally, there are the copays and coinsurance. If the cost of care comes in at $35,000, what's the patient's responsibility? Is it based on the bundled $45,000 payment or the actual cost? If the cost goes to $55,000 and the provider pays the difference, how does patient liability work?

Don't forget, it's not just humans who need to figure out this math and the process. Then we need to teach computers how to automate the rules to the millions of dollars of claims being submitted each day.

It's a rat's nest of complications, and the long-term investment and support simply aren't there to untangle them.

DOWNSIDE RISK

Imagine that an insurer actually gets an independent primary care provider to the deep end of the pool. Now they're taking on downside risk—and a situation arises where the insurer tells the provider that they owe it money.

They're an independent primary care provider. There's a shortage of PCPs in the United States. And now we're going to force this isolated PCP to pay the money back to the insurance carrier that's making millions in profits each year?

You're doing it to enforce behavior change, but it's going to have an unintended consequence. If it puts too much financial pressure on the PCP, as I described before, they're going to run for cover. If there's too much risk and it's too hard for them to administer, they're going to abandon their independent practice and become an employee of a larger provider group or health system. They can't deal with the downside anymore, and they reach for a lifeline. This lifeline ties back into the larger forces at play: negotiation weight between providers and insurers. Does an insurer really want to assist in the building of larger provider groups?

WHAT IT ALL MEANS

Aligning incentives around outcomes is an essential ingredient of the healthcare system we want, one that delivers high-quality care at an affordable price. But this goal can only be achieved as an element of a new system. It can't be achieved in isolation.

Imagine an employer who wants his workers to be on time, so he gives them each a Formula One race car. "I fixed it!" he says. "I got you a faster car so you can get to work on time!" But the speed limits, the roads, the traffic—none of that has changed. Sure, theoretically, it's a faster way to get to work. But it's simply not going to work in isolation.

What's an insurer to do? Well, if changing provider incentives doesn't work, how about influencing the choices the patients make?

CHAPTER 5

IF ONLY HEALTHCARE WERE SHOPPABLE

As value-based reimbursement became stuck in the shallow end of the pool, a new self-reform gained traction across the insurance industry: consumer choice architecture or, as its friends in the industry call it, benefit design.

Here's how I like to imagine its birth: picture yourself in a conversation at some boondoggle of a conference of insurance executives when someone has one glass of wine too many.

"You know what?" they say. "VBR isn't doing enough."

A colleague chimes in: "So, if it's not the providers' fault, then..."

Followed by everyone, all at once: "It must be the consumers' fault!"

Regardless of its true origins, benefit design is at least a straightforward concept. Insurers adjust their products to drive consumers to the lowest-cost, highest-quality care by erecting financial barriers—such as a high cost share for using out-of-network providers—intended to influence behavior. But what's simple conceptually doesn't stay that way. The manifestation of this understanding is the **Explanation of Benefits** (EOB), a detailed description of a complex tangle of incentivized coverage that everyone receives and no one grasps.

You might already be able to guess how well that's working.

DEFINITIONS

Again, let's define our terms.

Insurance Product: The specific coverage a consumer is entitled to, embodied in the insurance card they carry in their wallet, and what insurance benefits stand behind the ID number, group number, and often the RX number on the card.

Network: The providers a consumer has access to under their insurance coverage, locally and sometimes nationally, either In Network or Out of Network (OON).

These are the two dimensions of coverage in which the insurance industry's efforts to guide consumer choices are embodied.

PRODUCT PROFUSION

The first consequence of this approach was an outbreak of unique combinations of pharmacy benefits, provider networks, cost shares, and buy-ups. It's gotten away from us. I know of one payer with more than 10,000 product variants within a single state. That means one of their patients who comes to a provider may be covered under any one of 10,000 product variations. That one carrier may represent something like 10 to 30 percent of a provider's patient panel. Do the math. If other plans in that same state are similar, that suggests the provider may be dealing with somewhere between 35,000 to 100,000 total product variants across their entire panel. Most of these variations aren't things providers deal with on a day-to-day basis, but it still makes things complicated, especially when advising the patient on where to go to fill a prescription, for nonemergent imaging, or any other innocuous encounter that can turn into a devastating medical bill.

Each of these variants is designed with the goal of guiding the patient toward "better" healthcare decisions. That's the overarching goal. There are also plenty of products made with cost as the guiding light, informed by market intelligence telling the insurer that a lower price point is needed for a specific plan sponsor (employer client). But how is a patient to get the most out of their benefits, or a provider to manage their care, given the complexities of these programs? They're difficult enough for their creators to administer, let alone help guide a beneficiary toward understanding.

For example, one product might include a diabetes prevention program provided at no cost. If I'm a primary care doc and I'm dealing with a patient who is prediabetic, I'd love to enroll them in the program. But how the heck am I supposed to know if the patient is eligible for the free program, or if it's going to cost them a hundred bucks a month out of pocket? To be clear, the answer is that it is possible for the provider to answer any *single* question. The point I'm highlighting is the operational lift required for the day-to-day implementation of any one of these 10,000 good ideas.

EOB

The industry's answer to the operational challenge of choice architecture is the **Explanation of Benefits**. It's the document that details everything a consumer has purchased with their insurance plan. But it's pages long and, like the Terms of Service on a website, it's not often read and certainly not understood.

I'm basing this assertion purely on the thousand or so souls that I've met who work at health insurance companies and admit that they can't explain most of the terminology and coverage explanations in their own healthcare plan. They'll all quietly tell me, "Jeb, I've never read my EOB," or "I have no clue what it means." If the people working in the industry don't get it, there's no chance in hell that a layman will.

Imagine buying a phone plan and not knowing if data, texting, and your minutes are included—and not knowing how much it's going to cost, for that matter. On top of that, add this for stakes: how you use your phone is going to determine how you use a material percentage of your personal expenses. Oh, and how you use that phone plan is also going to be a matter of life and death.

Your insurance plan is one of the most expensive things you purchase. It's likely to be higher than your monthly car payment. If you're unhealthy or unlucky, it may be even higher than your mortgage. The same goes for most employers—it's the second- or third-largest line item on most balance sheets.

What have you purchased, exactly? What does it mean for you? It's all buried in your EOB.

SHOPABILITY

I talked in Chapter 2 about consumerism in healthcare and how the elements required for a successful free market simply don't exist in this sector of our economy. And yet the success of these products depends on consumerism—on the ability of patients to make informed choices about the care they receive, where and when they receive it, and its total cost.

Let's say I go to a primary care doctor in your community, and the cost under my plan is zero dollars. Cool, I can manage that.

But my plan also says that if I get my MRI at an outpatient facility, a community-based imaging center, my copay is twenty dollars. Or if I go to a hospital or a facility-based imaging center, it's going to cost two hundred bucks.

The plan is structured to guide me to the cheaper, community-based outpatient imaging center. But what if that center is quietly owned by a large health system? The signage won't necessarily reveal that. It's extremely challenging for me to know the right questions to ask to figure out the reality of my choice or, better yet, the cost of my choice.

What's more, when I'm in a healthcare setting, my consumer deflector shields are down. The basic dynamic between patient and provider is trust; it's the only way to close the vast gap in knowledge between the two participants in the conversation. A patient doesn't necessarily think of themselves as buying anything as a consumer at all. As a result, in the end, what the doctor says goes; even if the patient asks about cost, the provider may not know the answer. Consider the difference in mindset you'd bring through the doors of a car dealership. Shields up!

It's become so difficult for patients to navigate their own insurance plans that it's fostered the birth of a new industry dedicated to addressing—and profiting from—this problem. At its forefront is a company named Accolade, which went public at a valuation of $1.2 billion. Where to go for that MRI? Accolade will tell me. Should I get my glasses prescription filled at LensCrafters or Warby Parker? Where's the lowest copay for my blood-pressure pills? Accolade exists solely to answer these questions; the value it offers is an incredible improvement in the membership experience.

That's a sign of capitalism at work. Accolade is a great concept and a phenomenal company—but they're a by-product of a crappy system. It's a sign of a market filled with so much friction that it's impossible to navigate without help.

THE EVOLUTION OF PRODUCTS

In the 1980s, **Health Maintenance Organizations**

(HMOs) were all the rage. HMOs are gatekeepers, presenting consumers with a limited array of choices; minding the gate was your primary care physician, who controlled your access to any other health provider. HMOs feature lower monthly premiums and lower out-of-pocket limits than the alternative: PPOs, or **Preferred Provider Organizations.** Their costs are higher, but there's no longer a gatekeeper telling the patient if they can pass or where to go on the other side. PPOs evolved to offer the flexibility and freedom of choice that HMOs don't—and with time, they've become far more popular. Of course, that's not to say they're any more effective in delivering high-quality, low-cost care.

These are two of the largest delineations in product categories. (There is plenty of literature on product designs and a myriad of variations. I'm keeping it simple for the sake of argument.)

Another major delineation involves how a commercial client chooses to structure the coverage they buy. As employers struggle to keep their insurance costs down, we've seen an evolution from fully insured to level-funded plans. With fully insured plans, the insurance carrier bears almost all the risk, up or down. In simple terms, with a level-funded plan, if the costs over a fixed time frame are less than expected, the employer who purchased it gets a percentage of the unspent money back or credited. You can think of level-funded plans as the gateway drug to self-funding, or ASO plans, in which the employer bears most of the financial risk, while the insurance company is often reduced to simply providing the network of caregivers and adjudication of claims.

The final step in this evolution is the buy-up. These are bolt-on products a carrier will offer members or employers as add-ons to their product—such as telehealth, or a diabetes or COPD management program. All are offered to the employer at a fee that, from the carrier's point of view, makes things like the ASO products more profitable. The brokers who have emerged to guide employers through their product choices (speaking of signs of marketing inefficiencies) are incentivized to tailor a solution to a given client's complex healthcare benefits issues. That often leads to an assortment of buy-ups, a varied array of solutions cobbled together to get the best clinical and financial outcome for their employers. Of course, as in any service industry, the more complex you make your services and the administration of your ideas, the more essential you become. It's difficult to say if this is deliberately done by the broker to justify their own existence or is simply something that's needed due to the inefficiencies of the system. My sense is, like most industries, you have good apples and bad apples. I've seen brokers save clients millions, and I've seen brokers make millions.

For an employer facing a decision on coverage, what's the

tell on the value of buy-ups? Ask the carrier if they've incorporated the buy-up service into their fully insured book of business. Sometimes you'll find that they haven't. What does that mean? Perhaps that the insurance carrier itself doesn't believe in the value of the buy-up; if they did, they'd be using it with their fully insured clients, where the insurer bears the full financial liability and has every incentive to offer programs that are truly effective. (It can also mean that the insurance carrier already has a service similar to the buy-up that is inherently built into its fully insured offering. The point is: ask!)

HIGH-DEDUCTIBLE HEALTH PLANS

High-Deductible Health Plans (HDHPs) are structured to influence consumer choice in a most direct way: bearing financial costs. HDHPs typically put the consumer on the hook for the first $5,000 or $10,000 in costs outside of some free preventive care. Recently, we've seen the free services extended beyond your annual wellness check to more expensive services to ensure members are not delaying or avoiding necessary medical interventions. Nevertheless, the ultimate goal is to create a financial barrier that makes the patient become more of a "buyer" before utilizing care.

But we've already established that consumerism in healthcare doesn't actually exist. The system is simply too complex to navigate. EOBs are written to address people at between a third grade and fifth grade level of literacy. There is a reason for that: regulators have established that we have to ensure every beneficiary can read their benefits. It has to be very simple. Can you imagine explaining a high-deductible health plan to an eight- or nine-year-old? With $5,000 or $10,000 riding on how well they understand how to manage a very complicated insurance product? You wouldn't even attempt it. I'm sorry, but it just makes no sense.

Neither does the math. The median household savings in America is about $11,700 for a family of four. The average deductible for a family of four on an HDHP is about $12,000. So essentially what you're saying to the family is, "We're going to take all your savings before your health insurance kicks in—oh, and you'll pay us monthly for that privilege!" It's no wonder more than 75 percent of people with HDHPs never reach their deductible max. Either they're choosing not to spend their last dollar on medical care, or they don't have any dollars left.

VBID

The final frontier you'll hear about in product design is **Value-Based Insurance Design**, or VBID. This blends many components from both the provider and the patient side. It's an approach intended to drive patients and providers alike to high-value services while discouraging low-value services. In theory, it's on point. An annual wellness check is a high-value service, so it's offered at no cost. The financial barriers that might prevent a person from seeing their primary care doctor once a year are stripped away.

Where it gets tricky is in the more complicated spheres of medicine. What's high value to one patient might not be high value to another; VBID alone does almost nothing to make the healthcare system any more shoppable. And you very quickly come into conflict with the provider's clinical autonomy. They don't want to be told what they can and cannot do with every single patient, or adjust their treatment based on what an insurance carrier deems high versus low value.

It's very difficult to make a ubiquitous program work at scale, because at the scientific level, patients are different. The EOB is no easier to understand, the system no easier for the patient or the provider to navigate. So again, good luck!

NETWORKS

In theory, constraining the network of providers it accepts is one of the strongest carrots—and sticks, for that matter—an insurance company carries. But its effectiveness is constrained, first and foremost, by a market reality. Insurance carriers are graded on access. When they're trying to sell a product, the employer who's buying it is sure to ask what providers are included within the geographies that are relevant to them. If it's not high penetration and fails to provide access to a community's marquee providers, then who's going to buy it? So from the start, a carrier trying to influence choice by limiting the provider pool is at cross purposes with its own financial well-being. They have to have adequate networks to compete for business and anywhere access continues to be a trend. Unfortunately, this leads to almost every provider being credentialed with all major plans in a given market.

The problem with that? Imagine walking into a grocery store. You'd expect the store to make sure that all the food available is fresh, high quality, and priced appropriately. There's your shoppable experience. But if an insurance carrier ran the grocery store, you'd find a lot of stale food mixed in with the fresh, organic, healthy options. There'd be no marked prices, and the vegetables might be boxed or mislabeled so you can't even know what you're buying. Only after the fact would you know if the food you bought was actually good for you.

But of course we're talking about buying healthcare, not groceries. In terms of consequences, we're not talking about going home with stale food or coming down with indigestion; we're talking about life and death.

How does the insurance carrier attempt to fix that?

The response has been to create narrow networks—limiting the providers within their network—and making the case that they'll deliver higher quality at a lower cost. How do they sell that to providers? By saying, "While we'll pay you less, we'll guide you more business. What you lose in negotiating your unit cost down will result in your volume going up, up, up."

But "narrow" has a negative connotation, so the semantics of this approach had to change. Now they're framed as high-value or performance networks. "We're not reducing costs by constraining choice; we're curating value." Now the healthcare grocery store is a Trader Joe's or a Whole Foods. Or at least, that's what you're led to believe.

This too has not yielded the outcomes it's intended to produce. For one thing, hospitals themselves are among the largest employers an insurance company might serve as a commercial client in a given area. Can you imagine going to a large hospital and saying on the one hand, "You should buy my insurance product for your 38,000 employees," and on the other, "Sorry, but we're going to make you a tier-two provider, so it's going to cost more for patients to come to you than your competitor across the street."

What's that health system going to say to you? They're

definitely not going to buy your insurance product. Worse case, they get in bed with an insurance competitor of yours, negotiating a lower rate than the one you've negotiated with your tier-one provider in the region. There are times when the by-product of this—lower rates—are positive for the employer and the patient, but most often, they're not.

So here's what happens: narrow networks aren't actually all that narrow. Healthcare remains unshoppable. It remains too difficult to evaluate and navigate choices based on medical necessity, cost, and quality.

First stop for the self-reform train: change provider incentives—sounded awesome! That didn't work.

Second stop: change individual consumer choices—oh, this is interesting! Didn't work either.

What's next? Let's "fix" the population as a whole.

CHAPTER 6

PROFITABILITY MEETS POPULATION HEALTH

"Instead of war on poverty, they got a war on drugs so the police can bother me."

—TUPAC SHAKUR

Of all the insurance industry's self-reforms, **Population Health Management** (PHM) comes closest to cracking the nut. Attempting to change provider behavior through VBR and then consumer choices through product and network structures both fell short; they were partial measures creating incremental improvements that barely beat inflation rates, at their best, and were doomed to fail in the tangle of incentives and complexities that bind our healthcare system. They were Band-Aids placed on a tumor.

PHM is different, at least in theory. It's a reform based on improving the population's health as a whole by addressing the social determinants that shape our well-being. It's certain to be an essential block in the foundation of our *next* healthcare system—but in the context of our current system, PHM hasn't moved the needle enough.

We are seeing more investments in this area, and I have nothing but admiration for those who are pursuing the promise with all their hearts. But don't mistake this commitment for evidence that someone has finally cracked the nut. If there's a real ROI to be had in PHM today, it's probably in the realm of optics and earned media coverage—here we are, out in the community, being good Samaritans—rather than anything based on actual results.

Do payer-sponsored PHM programs improve lives? Yes. Do they do enough to change the broader trajectory of our healthcare sector? No.

In the context of our current system, and for all the good intentions behind it, PHM is just one more step on the road to nowhere of industry self-reform. Like the others we've already discussed, it's not leading us anywhere near term—not beyond the valuable lessons it's providing for our future-state rebuild. (That's where we're headed in Part 3.)

For now let's start by exploring the meaning and promise of PHM, and the reasons it's falling short.

THE POTENTIAL IN POPULATION HEALTH

There are, I think, three core components to health: being *mentally, physically,* and *emotionally* balanced. It's a holistic picture. If I wake up at 5 a.m., listen to some good music, and eat a healthy breakfast, I'm going to feel ready for a run. How we feel determines what we do, and that leads to what we become.

When I see someone walking down the street—a stranger, a friend—who strikes me as healthy, I don't typically think, *Oh my gosh, they must have such a great doctor!* What I'm more likely to think is that they eat pretty well, they work out, they've got a decent job with a reliable income, they're well educated, and they're surrounded by a supportive group of people. They know how to navigate everything from a supermarket to their personal life, and they're managing the stresses and bad habits that can lead to health issues. Their socioeconomics are strong and so are they.

The opposite is true too. When I see someone who's unhealthy, I don't think, *My god! Their doctor must be horrible!*

That simple observation is really enough to validate the importance of PHM. It is the right focus if your goal is to improve the health of people across the population. Research backs it up. Numerous studies over the past ten to twenty years have confirmed that 90 percent of what affects any individual's healthcare status is dependent on socioeconomic factors, with only 10 percent impacted by the care you receive.

The question at the heart of PHM is how we can help a patient help themselves. As the research makes clear, the answer lies outside the walls of the doctor's office and the hospital.

PHM shifts the focus to the root causes of healthy behavior. By leveraging large swaths of data from public and private sources, it moves you away from a reactive change-things-at-the-point-of-care mentality—which is the focus of self-reforms that have come before—to look upstream. Instead of capturing patients with mismanaged diabetes in the emergency room for avoidable issues, capture them "upstream" with an education program on prediabetes management. Don't just shift the incentives around the ER visit; avoid it altogether.

The implications for insurers are broad. Instead of focusing simply on clinical care, look to the causal pathways that lead to so many acute and costly healthcare problems. Stretch the focus to jobs, housing, education, cultural and geopolitical norms—the underlying realities that govern the decisions we all make as individuals.

This can only be done effectively at the local level, because in the end, our lives are local, so healthcare must be too.

There's research that shows a person's zip code is more predictive of their health status than their genetic code. It's stunning, but it's true. So if you're serving a community where everyone is supposed to clean their plate, and their plate is heaped with saturated fats and high fructose corn syrup, that's a place to start.

The converse is true too. A big insurance company that deploys a statewide program that rewards thirty minutes of cardiovascular exercise is going to fail the plausibility test in a neighborhood where there's no opportunity to get 10,000 steps. That's simply going to marginalize the marginalized while rewarding the Fitbit crew that has a steady income and child care. They're usually the demographic that really doesn't need another thirty-dollar discount on their premium.

Still, the promise is there. PHM is one of the most worthwhile initiatives health insurers could undertake—and many of them are. The dollars they're investing are serious; you'll often see PHM leadership vested at the vice-presidential level.

It's probably worth noting that I'm a human nutrition, foods, and exercise major from Virginia Tech. I was excited when PHM became a thing in the insurance industry. *Finally!* I thought. *I'm about to begin to capture some return on my four years of out-of-state tuition!*

WHY HASN'T IT WORKED?

It would be encouraging, in a sense, if there were a single reason why PHM programs have fallen short of their promise. But I see at least six.

SEEING ISN'T FIXING

PHM requires that you address the root cause, not simply identify it—and insurance companies have proven much better at the latter than the former.

Insurers are terrific at analytics. They're well equipped to synthesize large data sets and predict healthcare outcomes based on that information. For example, if you were to string all the publicly available data together, you might find that if someone's a forty- to fifty-year-old African American in downtown Los Angeles who's been arrested for a drug-related misdemeanor in the last two years and filed for Section 8 housing in the previous year, there is a one-in-three chance that they'll end up in the emergency room in the next ninety days.

That's great. You've essentially identified a causal pathway. It's the first step and it's critical. But that's not fixing anything. If the data is not translated into effective action, it's not leading anywhere. How do you engage all the beneficiaries who match your predictive analytics, and what is the appropriate action?

THE LIMITS OF SELF-INTEREST

Some of the nicest people I've met in the industry are leaders of nonprofit foundations established by insurance companies to make local advancements to address social issues related to health. They lead to things like 5K walks, neighborhood cleanups, and food banks. I don't mean to call them out; I appreciate what they do.

But they're aligning their efforts around their organization's priorities, not necessarily the community's. The company is using its tax-free assets to decide what is needed in the community. If they deploy social workers and nutritionists to run a diabetes prevention program or free nutritional counseling on one side of the city, what's happening on the other? Why diabetes and not congestive heart failure or COPD?

In addition, when you have multiple plans each choosing their own community strategy rather than a unified approach, we miss a critical opportunity to leverage scale and long-term sustainability—qualities that so many PHM programs lack.

When the insurer's priorities and the community's are aligned, great. But who's voting on where or how they spend this money? No one from the public. It's a private organization. The intentions are good, but the results are a patchwork approach driven by self-interest that can often perpetuate inequity, not fix it. It's not an unsolvable problem—again, Part 3, it's coming!—but that's today's reality.

THE SLOW PACE OF RETURNS

Insurance companies commonly think in one- to two-year returns on their investments, especially when it comes to patient interventions. Twelve to twenty-four months is typically all they've got to capture the ROI. That's not due to the cost of the investment itself. It's because payers have to consider the churn of their beneficiaries; if the participants in your diabetes prevention program move to another insurer, then your competitor gets the benefit of your investment. They're the ones now insuring the healthier patient who's making good nutritional decisions and accounting for less medical and prescription spending.

There's only one instance when that's not the case: an insurance company with a very large market share and a population that's unlikely to move in and out of their coverage. If you own 80 to 90 percent of a Medicaid market, you might retain those patients for as long as they're on Medicaid. Granted, that's not necessarily the most lucrative market segment. But you can afford to make investments into the community because those patients will be with you years down the road when a safer living environment with a stable job finally leads to lower avoidable utilization and higher health plan returns. You'll enjoy the benefits that you wouldn't with a smaller market share and higher member churn.

THE WRONG AGENTS OF CHANGE

When's the last time you really engaged with your insurance company? I got something in the mail from my local insurance company the other day, and I didn't even open it. I didn't know what they were pushing, but I knew it didn't hit my top three priorities for the day. I left it on my kitchen table for a week before I finally threw it out. If there's a message on my phone from a nurse or a social worker from the insurance company, I'm not returning it. If I'm calling back anybody who calls about my health, it's my local provider, because that's who I've developed a relationship with.

True agents of change come from within the community. They don't drop in by parachute. One program in South America set out to teach people to boil water before they drank it, killing the parasites that were making them sick. They deployed their program, did their education outreach... and nothing changed. The people they were there to help kept getting sick. Finally, they went to a local woman (a change agent in disguise) and asked, "What are we doing wrong?"

"It's simple," she said. "We boil water to clean dead bodies before they go to burial; to us, boiling water signifies preparing for death."

They were completely missing the mark. Their science was correct, but they failed to understand the community dynamics that governed the decisions they were trying to influence.

A related challenge is actually reaching the people you need to reach. We're talking about needier populations here, not the Fitbit crew who are actively engaged in their own health and check their patient portal every week. The people PHM programs need to reach are often bumping in and out of government assistance programs. They run out of minutes on their phone every month. They're not checking their email because they don't have email, or physical mail for that matter. Simply communicating with the people you're trying to reach is very difficult—especially if you're a parachuter just dropping in.

I can't stress enough the need to get out in the communities you serve and truly understand the human behaviors that are leading to the outcomes you're trying to change.

When I oversaw value-based strategy for a large regional health plan, I took members of my team into the community. We went to a lower-income part of town, and I asked them to get out of the car, go into the local corner store, and convince the next patron who walked in to buy water instead of soda or to not buy the candy bar, cigarettes, or day-old pizza they had selected. They could use any tactic they wanted.

Surely if you're good enough to develop a value-based reimbursement model that impacts millions of dollars of spent, you can get one person to change their decision that day...

We counted twenty-seven people over forty-five minutes, and guess what? Only one person changed their behavior, and that was when I offered the cashier ten dollars to give away two waters in exchange for the next soda purchase. The cashier convinced an older woman to make the deal.

Never underestimate your agents of change!

BAD HABITS

The unfortunate fact is that many people, despite enduring major healthcare challenges, still don't engage in healthy behavior. You can attribute that to any number of factors, from personal motivation to broader dynamics, but it's simply fact.

One study of heart attack survivors found that one year after their crisis, less than half were adhering to their medication regimen. A heart attack is one of the scariest episodes a person will ever face; the most important organ in your body is failing. And just a year out, less than half are taking medicine they need to help prevent it from happening again. That's telling.

If you think a simple email or a text or a voice message is

going to change someone's behavior when a heart attack doesn't, I'm hard-pressed to believe you're right.

BAD INFLUENCES

We live our lives within a broader framework that governs our choices and shapes our thinking. PHM programs are fighting behaviors that are created and supported by much more well-funded and deeply rooted influencers. For more than forty years, the International Olympic Committee was sponsored by McDonald's. What the hell? You're telling me that the healthy behavior of elite Olympic athletes is based on McDonald's? When you put the Olympics and McDonald's together, don't you think the kids notice? That's the whole point from the McDonald's point of view.

Tupac had it right. We're fighting the war on drugs, but it's the wrong war. Fight poverty, and drug use will surely drop with it.

Programs alone—even good programs—aren't enough. We need to change the societal frameworks too.

I know I'm being simplistic, but the fact that so many PHM programs don't account for this makes me think that it needs to be stated.

THE PERSISTENT PROMISE

I don't want to leave you with the impression that PHM programs are doomed to fail. Of all the elements of self-reform, they're among the most compelling. There are success stories in spite of all the factors working against them that I've described. I'll look at those more closely in Part 3, when we turn to describing the elements of a new and more effective healthcare system.

For now, I'll leave it at this: PHM programs that work harness the power in local agents of change, and they're characterized by a payer-agnostic approach to financial returns. They typically focus on populations of need, which aren't the high-margin commercial clientele. There are also plenty of wellness programs in the commercial space, but let's just say it's easier for me to solve world hunger than to defend the efficacy of many of these.

I'm not making a statement based on politics. I try to speak only from math and common sense. If we don't invest in taking care of the people who can't afford insurance, they will inevitably utilize care, most likely in an acute state that could have been avoided because, say, their untreated hypertension has resulted in a stroke. They'll land in an expensive facility that will realize this as uncompensated care. Eventually, that facility will cross-subsidize, offsetting its loss through higher reimbursement rates from commercial clients or government relief programs.

If you have a job or pay taxes, you will eventually pay to provide care for our most needy populations regardless of whom you vote for. PHM programs hold the promise of paying less by intervening earlier, proactively avoiding costs while doing the right thing for your fellow man and woman. It's that rare instance: investing in PHM makes both moral and financial sense. We're just not going about it the right way—yet.

CHAPTER 7

NECESSITY IS THE MOTHER OF INNOVATION

"If I had asked people what they wanted, they would have said a faster horse."

—A QUOTE INCORRECTLY ATTRIBUTED TO HENRY FORD, BUT A FITTING QUOTE NONETHELESS

With the string of self-reform attempts I've documented so far, the insurance industry is running out of levers to pull. As with population health management, the last one it's got—innovation—has promise. But much of what passes for innovation in the industry doesn't go deep enough.

It's difficult for any industry to rise above the inevitable restraint of "If it ain't broke (for us), don't fix it." Organizations are inherently biased against potentially undermining their own profitability, even if they can see that, eventually, the revenue-generating model they depend on is on the verge of breaking the American family bank account. So what you're left with are efforts to modernize and digitize a broken system toward success—a system that simply can't deliver on the twin goals of higher-quality care at an affordable cost that we're chasing.

In Chapter 6, I wrote of how my enthusiasm for population health management was based on my undergraduate degree in human nutrition, food, and exercise from Virginia Tech. Well, here we go again: I followed that degree with a few other complementary degrees and eventually a master's in health care innovation (MHCI), then a new program at Penn. And what I can tell you, by virtue of my education and my experience since, is that when it comes to innovation, most organizations—especially insurers—are missing the point.

TO FOLLOW OR LEAD?

The quote that opens this chapter—logically though apparently incorrectly attributed to Henry Ford, the architect of the first great "horseless carriage," the Model T—speaks to a cognitive dissonance at the heart of innovation practices: Who's the innovator anyway? Does the customer know what they need, or do we in the business know better? It's not dissimilar from many other paternalistic questions in healthcare: If the doctor knows best, then do we even need to consider the patient's perspective? Sometimes it's the insurance carrier that "knows best" and makes decisions that have dramatic impacts on employers. Often it can even be the broker or consultant who decides what the employer needs and what the insurance companies should do about it. This counterbalance and decision ownership issue is ubiquitous in healthcare.

Argue from the customer's point of view, and you'd say every beneficiary can tell you how they want healthcare to evolve; just listen. Argue from the industry's point of view, and you'd say that beneficiaries have no idea what they want and that we're the ones who have to drive the market forward, that only the industry visionary can see all the chess pieces and play the game at the macro level.

Do you respond to what the market's asking for? Maybe it's limited by what the average patient can even imagine possible? Or do you trust that you're the visionary, doing your best to be the Elon Musk of health insurance, not just reading the market but leading it?

Regardless of your point of view, you'll typically find a company's ambitions for change embodied in a chief innovation officer, chief strategy officer, or even a chief digital officer responsible for thinking about what the world looks like five years from now and working to ensure that every initiative aligns with that vision.

THE SCIENCE OF INNOVATION

Innovation is about much more than a spark of imagination, the work of a creative genius sequestered in a lab somewhere. Believe it or not, there's a new and ever-deepening scientific understanding of innovation captured in textbooks and studies and frameworks for change. My go-to reference is a book called *Universal Methods of Design*, which outlines more than one hundred "progressive design frameworks." These are choice architectures—different formulaic approaches—to solving complex problems.

A core element of these frameworks is human-centered design. Your goal in innovating is not to make things better for machines or computers or algorithms, but instead to make the systems and tools we rely on better serve the needs of people. Everything from the experience to the outcome is captured in these progressive design frameworks, forcing healthcare stakeholders to humanize their science-first approaches.

As a result, good design thinking begins with empathy: understanding what the person is dealing with. Then you define the problem, and only then do you ideate solutions, prototype, and test. That's the framework for beginning to innovate.

A similar science is evolving around motivational design—the process of motivating people to change not through charismatic interventions but through a systemic approach. Ways to better influence students to learn or employees to work. How do you begin to guide people through new choice architectures? How do you think about solving complex issues with formulaic approaches?

These methodological approaches to innovation are often underappreciated in the healthcare industry, a sector oriented toward protecting many of the archaic processes that, ironically, are the reasons there's an unequivocal need for innovation in the first place.

I'm not arguing against the need to embrace the science of innovation in healthcare. I'm not arguing against the executive positions that are responsible for this process either. But I do have reservations. I knew a colleague who joked about how "innovation" should never appear in a job title because everyone should be thinking about how to improve the system, or at least their role in it. He's right; innovation *should* be part of everyone's job.

In an ideal environment, everyone would be a champion of continuous performance improvement, and there would be no need for a deliberate focus on innovation. But most people who work in the industry are entirely focused on their silo, their "nine to five," absorbed in keeping the machine rolling. That doesn't mean they're intentionally perpetuating inefficiencies; it's simply that they have a job to do. They don't have the time or the ability to step back and question why the process works the way it does or ideate on a plan for the future. You need an entrusted few to look at the overall system and identify areas of opportunity for improvement.

The question is where they're focused and to what end.

INTERNAL REALITIES

When most people think about innovation, they think about creating something entirely new. Putting turbochargers on engines to make cars go faster was not nearly as innovative as developing engines to begin with.

Choosing the term *innovation* to describe a department or initiative may lead people to believe that you've dedicated an entire division to working tirelessly on the future, but that's not often what's happening under the innovation umbrella that the insurance industry is now holding over its head.

I know people who are leading these efforts at a lot of health plans and health systems, and they're doing great work. But the fact is that they're often focused on optimization—turbochargers, not entirely new ways of getting from here to there.

There's a good reason for this. Inefficiency in the healthcare system accounts for nearly a trillion dollars in spending every year. That's over one dollar in every three spent in this country on healthcare. Seem impossible? Think of yourself as a patient. Consider everything from the way your claim is processed by your insurer, clinical mistakes related to diagnosis, coding, and corresponding treatment, or when your independent physician can't access the results of a recent diagnostic you had at a neighboring facility, so they repeat the lab. These workflow inefficiencies also create opportunities for fraud and abuse as wrongdoers play in the loopholes.

As a result, innovation teams are often focused on improving existing workflows rather than creating new workflows altogether. I used to be that guy, actually, arguing for incremental improvement rather than a complete overhaul. After all, overhauls require serious capital, many years, and a ton of corporate trust and buy-in. The inevitable result is usually a sequence of small improvements in how an engine runs, with no one challenging the way the engine was built in the first place—because that would throw off the economic horsepower that the engine generates.

These improvements, of course, are internal to the organization that's developing them. Their influence is narrow because the result is greater efficiency for the organization itself. There is nothing wrong with that; what's more efficient for the organization—such as an automated system for prior authorization taking five minutes instead of five days—can help the provider and patient too.

Sometimes the changes are big, such as enterprise overhauls of very complex systems of record, claims processing units, or even provider credentialing processes. The obstacle to this level of change is that these systems are often built on top of each other like bricks in a wall; you can't change one without addressing a myriad of interdependencies involving other systems that feed or get fed by one you're trying to change. That leads to a myriad of judgments involving more than technical knowledge, leaving only a few folks who know why something was done this way and not the other way. We like to call that "institutional knowledge," which is polite, but I prefer to call it "technical job security." And in the end, by and large, even these big changes are made in the name of optimization and efficiency, not the sort of revolutionary change we associate with technology.

In theory, these efficiencies should lead to higher profit margins, which *should* result in lower premiums. I do believe insurer margins are scrutinized—the pressures insurers face from employers who pay the bills are real—but we really haven't yet seen that translate into dramatically lower premiums or even encouraging trends. One reason is the optimization effort required to fix the underlying system (these initiatives are often labeled "innovation enablers") before you can get to the fun stuff of building something creative, beneficial, and member-facing on top of it.

As I've said, I had "innovation" in my job title more than once and have had it in almost every job description in my career. In one of these roles in particular, I truly believed I was being entrusted with guiding the organization into the future as a new entity. That just wasn't the case. The vast majority of my time was absorbed in internal operational improvements. I'd venture to say that less than 10 percent of my time was free to focus on dreaming up new ways of doing things to drive higher-quality results at lower costs.

Perhaps you read that and are thinking, *Well, that's just a symptom of poor management or the lack of an overarching strategy.* But I can assure you that anyone that has been in a similar position knows that you need both short- and long-term results. And when you're long on strategy and short on execution, you realize that incremental improvement is better than nothing at all.

In most circumstances, that sliver of time focused on ideation has nothing to do with clinical innovation—actually working with providers to change the ways we deliver care. You're with an insurer, not a health system. As we discussed in the case of VBR, insurers do hold great influence—they control the money—and can theoretically bend clinician and patient behaviors using an array of tactics. But in reality, as I've outlined, there is a complex dance between providers and payers, and it often supports the status quo.

The risk to the carrier in disrupting that dance to drive innovation is just too high. Far easier than exposing that uncomfortable relationship to scrutiny and bad publicity is simply shrugging it away: We're only representing a small portion of the provider's patient panel, their total book, and we really don't have enough leverage to make them practice medicine differently.

The exception that proves what is to this point, a rule, is the emergence and propagation of **Integrated Delivery and Financing Systems** (IDFS). This is when a health insurance company and a healthcare provider, typically a large health system or network of providers, come together under one broader entity: Kaiser Permanente, Intermountain Healthcare, Highmark. This phenomenon of shared accountability for clinical outcomes and cost of the patients is also seen in provider-sponsored health plans, accountable care organizations, patient-centered medical homes, and other risk-bearing entities that expose providers to the financial outcomes of their clinical decisions. What all these initiatives have in common is this: they're innovation teams that can play on both sides of the fence, dealing with both insurance and delivery of care.

VENTURE CAPITAL

It's common to find venture capital dollars floating around or near the innovation team. This is true not only in insurance but also with providers, pharmaceuticals, consultancies, and technology companies. Insurance companies are taking some of their proceeds and investing them—betting on—small companies that are attempting to drive disruptive changes. That's a form of innovation, right? Diversifying revenue streams while investing in others who are innovating?

What's interesting to me is that insurers have the ability to take that company they've invested in and push it toward their clients. If they invest in a technology company or care management company, they can use their brand and relationships to push that company into the market—serving as a channel partner. Their clients might not even know that the insurance company has a financial interest in the product they're pushing.

Most healthcare startups are dying for the validation and credibility such an investment can bring. Startups are acutely aware of the group-think mentality in healthcare; if a big insurer "signs off" by striking a deal with them, it sends a legitimizing signal to the entire market—so much so that the startups will often offer material discounts if that's the price of winning the right to publish and announce the partnership. I negotiated these contracts when I was in the startup world, and believe me, insurers are well aware of this leverage, and they use it.

I think of this as the dark side of the innovation coin, and I have to confess I've had a hand in it. I once had an insurer client that had invested in a startup focused on value-based care management of a pervasive chronic disease. The insurer was worried that its employer clients would throw a fit if the insurer added a new line item on their monthly billing statement to cover this startup's service. So the insurer assisted the startup in aligning its services to a specific CPT code that the innovator could use to bill for its service, allowing the insurer to tuck it into the very large line item of monthly medical expenses. This is perfectly legal and a rational strategy for a number of reasons. The insurance company grilled the startup on its ability to deliver value, as it should—I'm talking over a year of diligence—and made it very clear they'd have to defend that value if the bill was ever challenged. But in essence, it kept the full truth out of view of the brokers and employers who administered and paid the bill. The insurer certainly wasn't pushing snake oil, but they were doing all they could to give their investment a frictionless path to profitability.

Some insurance divisions actually have enough money right now, and enough clout with their clients, that they're hiring **Entrepreneurs in Residence**, or EIRs, to build companies within their broader insurance company. The insurer provides the marketing, legal, and overhead support the EIR needs to build out their idea, and it's built under the umbrella of the broader insurance company. The insurance company is serving as a startup incubator and taking a fixed percentage of equity and/or royalties for its support.

To me, these efforts amount to a confession where the insurance company is truly showing its cards. They're acknowledging that they're not fit for the future, and they need unique divisions and strategies to develop the big, broad, new ideas that are being demanded. It makes business sense, but you have to know these EIRs are also informed of the sacred animals in the business model, the areas that they can't disrupt. Insurers want to market and show that they're "trailblazing" but not trailblazing so fast that they work their way out of a job.

I used to think of innovation divisions as the most honest in terms of insurers recognizing the need to fight for relevance in the future of healthcare delivery. But as you begin to peel apart the onion and identify where you find waste, where there are avoidable costs, you begin to take your eye off the provider and focus on the transactional partners, who often appear as middlemen.

And in this case, the middleman is very far from the middle. In fact, it happens to sit at the top of the totem pole.

CHAPTER 8

THE WHOLE IS NOT GREATER THAN THE SUM OF ITS PARTS

"The point is, ladies and gentlemen, that greed, for lack of a better word, is good."

—ACTOR MICHAEL DOUGLAS AS THE UNSCRUPULOUS BROKER GORDON GEKKO IN *WALL STREET*

Can you imagine what would happen, after a decade of self-reform, if oil companies said "Look, we know gas is fifteen dollars a gallon and your cars are still stalling on the side of the road, but trust us, 2022 is our year!" Or coffee shops, promising change at last after a decade of increasing prices by 5 percent a year for a bitter brew? We would never put up with it.

And yet we do with healthcare. The insurance industry has been rolling out self-reforms for years now, and they've done all but nothing to address our poor outcomes and high costs. In fact, when you add up all the industry's ideas, all its well-intended initiatives, the sum is actually more inefficiencies and a more expensive system.

The evidence is in: trusting the insurance industry to self-reform has resulted in poorly executed strategies and disappointing results, governed not by any overarching vision but by the industry's own inertia. The influences and incentives that drive insurance companies have made their efforts to self-reform self-defeating. It doesn't help that the broader healthcare sector is completely implicated in this; politicians, health systems, and many other stakeholders have aided and abetted in this half-pregnant effort.

PROGRESS OR PROMOTION?

It's now reached the point that "fixing the system" has become more of a marketing tagline than a strategy. I've been in healthcare for more than a decade, and every year brings the breathless introduction of exciting new initiatives that promise revolutionary change, increasing the quality of care, decreasing the cost, and propelling us into the future.

Spend a few minutes with Google Search, and you'll see

what I mean. I played around with "2020 health insurance" and came up with more than twenty reform initiatives announced by regional and national insurance carriers. The top terms for 2020 seemed to be "reimagined," "reengineered," "reset," and my favorite, "Healthcare 2.0." We're only getting to 2.0 now? There must be a lot of versions to the second decimal out there—1.01, 1.92, etc.—and I'm finding them still very buggy!

Fixing the system is not a strategy. It's a schtick.

What the hell have you been doing for the past decade, industry? Never mind the decades before—what have you been doing over just the last ten years?

Let me support my point by borrowing a lesson from Dr. Zeke Emmanuel, my department chair at Penn. He asked us what year and what president of the United States said this:

> Adequate emphasis should be given to facilities that are particularly useful for prevention of diseases—mental as well as physical—and to the coordination of various kinds of facilities. It should be possible to go a long way toward knitting together facilities for prevention with facilities for cure, the large hospitals of medical centers with the smaller institutions of surrounding areas, the facilities for the civilian population with the facilities for veterans.

It's all there: mental health, prevention, coordination and navigation of healthcare, and so on. It feels current; it seems as if it could have been any president over the past few decades. So who said it?

Here's a hint: it's the president who convinced the country that dropping two atomic bombs was warranted but couldn't get universal healthcare passed.

You've got it! Harry Truman, 1945.

A quote more than seventy-five years old remains our industry's party line today. Come on!

Why, now, all of a sudden, can the industry claim to have figured out something it didn't know nine—or seventy-five—years ago? Why should we continue to pay for innovation divisions and massive consultancies that turn around and say, "*Now* we've got something better up our sleeves"?

Really? Now? Does this really reflect an open-minded effort to rethink healthcare, or is it an exercise in repositioning in continuing to deflect the pressure that continues to build from employers whose business is burdened by the ever-rising cost of insurance for their employees? Is the real message "Let's change this," or is it "Please bear with us as we figure ourselves out, because there has to be a better future out there somewhere"?

Here's the problem. It's only going to get worse. An aging population means more people moving onto government-sponsored plans. And as I've discussed, these are not the profit segments providers yearn for; instead, they often have to cross-subsidize these patients by charging higher fees to their commercial populations. What happens when the ratio of people on commercial plans compared to government plans continues to fall?

Our geriatric population as a percentage of our total population will increase by more than thirty percent over the next two decades—and it will break the commercial cross-subsidization game!

We're at a tipping point, and the macroeconomics are increasing the pressure for insurers to solve this issue, and fast.

Here's what would show me that insurance carriers are willing to move beyond bullshit and live by their latest slogans: they'd price forward on their latest initiatives.

What I mean by that is that when a company rolls out an initiative and says it's expected to reduce costs by 10 percent, then they'd drop their premiums by 10 percent at the same time. Right? If you truly believe in your promotion, drop your prices now, not later.

That's not how carriers traditionally do business—not unless they've negotiated a concrete, absolute 10 percent reduction by, say, renegotiating pharmaceutical costs with the manufacturer or the **Pharmacy Benefits Manager** (PBM), or reduced the unit cost on a provider's reimbursement.

It's as if I promised to write you one hundred emails every day for one hundred dollars with this pitch: just give me the money upfront, and I'll do my best to give you your one hundred emails. Would you accept that? Of course not. You'd pay me a dollar an email, and probably only after all services are rendered.

When an insurance company says, "Hey, we've got a great new idea!" and they won't price for it, it makes you wonder whether the strategies were ever intended to work to begin with.

Consider how much more meaningful it would be to hear this: "Hey, we're going to provide a discount this year because we know this strategy is going to work!"

I'm not saying it's a case of maliciousness. It's more a matter of masking self-doubt, of making believe all is well instead of asking deep questions. "Look at providers," they're saying, "look at consumers, look at our competitors, look at our population, our society—just don't look at us, because we're well intended, and we're doing our best."

It's easier that way. As President George W. Bush once said in addressing latent prejudice: "Too often, we judge other groups by their worst examples, while judging ourselves by our best intentions."

JOBBED

One key measure of the failure of self-reform is employment. In any other sector, true innovation typically involves the elimination of archaic jobs. That's why we don't have many train conductors anymore or manufacturing jobs. It's both progress and a problem, but it's a measure of true change.

Healthcare employment is projected to increase by more than 15 percent over the next ten years, according to the U.S. Bureau of Labor Statistics. This far outpaces any other industry—and keep in mind, healthcare already employs almost one in seven people working in the United States today.

We typically don't see the elimination of archaic jobs in the health insurance industry. Instead, we see new jobs being added while archaic jobs remain. It's a universal problem. Wherever I go in the country and whoever I talk to, everyone seems to be struggling with the upskilling issue. They're stymied by the worker who's fifty or fifty-five and dragging their feet because they're closing in on retirement and don't want to go get an associate's degree now or bother with a new skillset. Force the issue, and you face a mass uprising; lay them off, and you face an uproar. If the people understood that by firing a thousand people who lack the right skillset an insurer could reduce premiums, they might feel differently about it. But they don't understand that. The system is too complex, and the insurer has no incentive to force the issue.

The result? We see new hires for new skills.

Let me show you what I mean with several examples. I'm generalizing a bit, but I think these are more the rule than the exception.

VBR

In Chapter 4, I talked about Value-Based Reimbursement (VBR)—the effort to shift providers from a Fee-for-Service (FFS) to an outcome-based model. For insurance carriers, putting this into practice required new negotiating skills with providers.

Under the FFS model, the insurer's contracting team focused on unit cost: the lower they drove cost in negotiations with providers, the better. I've worked with people who have fifteen to twenty years of experience in FFS contract negotiations, and with that experience, they've developed the skills required to do their job well. They've also developed relationships with providers that are a great asset in and of themselves.

But negotiating a VBR contract requires new negotiation skills. It's a much more complicated formula than unit cost and volume, with a lot more put-and-takes.

As a result, you'd expect a new job profile, encompassing not just the old skills but the new ones too. You'd expect retraining and upskilling, equipping your contract team to strike a new type of bargain without sacrificing the provider relationships they've developed.

Unfortunately, that's not what we've seen to date. Instead, you see new jobs for value-based specialists on contracting teams. You've added more people to the equation without removing others or, at the very least, ensuring that greater value has been created.

CLINICAL TRANSFORMATION TEAMS

Negotiating a VBR deal is one thing; guiding providers on transforming clinical operations to support moving from the shallow end of the pool to the deep end is another. The result: the clinical transformation resource, often added to provider relation teams just as VBR negotiators are added to contract teams.

Provider teams still employ their old-school people, who are masters of the world of unit-cost relationships and have long-standing relationships that create the trust these new reimbursement models require. Once again, we don't often see a new job profile written to address both old skills and new. We don't see efforts to upskill existing workers or eliminate archaic jobs. Instead, we see new folks added to an existing team, complementing the team rather than rethinking it.

THE A(P)I

How many times have we heard that technology is going to propel us into a new world of healthcare? Save us money? Make things more efficient? Drive better results? It's what we've seen in almost every other sector transformed by technology.

Healthcare is, without a doubt, extremely complex. A typical insurance company has so many technology platforms, it would be hard-pressed to count them. Given that, a key to technological innovation is interoperability—integrating the systems seamlessly and efficiently, which includes technologies that are both internal and external to the insurer.

The most common tool for the job is what's known as an API (for **Application Program Interface**), a standardized mechanism that allows different platforms to exchange information. The healthcare standard for exchanging data is called "fire," for **Fast Healthcare Interoperability Resources** (FHIR). With the FHIR API, different organizations could roll out different types of technology, and the one guarantee is that they'd all be able to interact with each other.

With FHIR, integration should be a step process. The whole point is to make the Lego bricks easy to connect. But instead, it's become a new full-time job. For every new technology, every new interface with providers, there's seemingly a new job. Now the provider that's committed to Cerner or Epic or another eight-figure electronic health record system needs someone to write the API that connects with the insurers, the vendors, and the insurer needs the same. And we all know the current APIs are an incremental step toward interoperability—data flows, but it is still limited in its functional use, given how it's structured and whether the data can even be placed in discrete fields.

It's not letting air out of the healthcare cost balloon. It's blowing air in and then squeezing it.

Within healthcare at least, API has been misnamed. It's not an Application *Program* Interface. It's an Application *People* Interface, and it's pulling more people into the cost equation.

I won't go deeply into how technology has also been a core

driver in dissatisfaction for many of our clinician partners—but trust me, it's not efficient, and it's not meaningfully improving experiences, as it promised.

THE UPSKILLING CHALLENGE

It should be clear by now that I believe existing teams can be—and need to be—upskilled to drive the efficiencies we should expect from innovation. It's an assumption and not something I can prove, but I believe they must be.

This is not to say I believe it's easy. I've worked inside insurance branches. I've met the fifty-five-year-old who spent twenty-five years as a claims and billing specialist. I've also met the twenty-five-year-old who just got their associate's degree in medical billing and is certainly not planning to go right back to school again. I've met the managers, directors, and VPs, and I've seen how defensive they all are of the status quo. I know how much they don't want to change or to learn a new skillset. I know how much they don't know about the term *automation* and yet how much they fear the very word.

The reality is that not everyone can adapt to change. It's also true that we don't have the programs in place to help organizations take these people and upskill them. Not every employee can and will adapt, but we can't simply let organizations take the easy way out and just add new jobs to the old.

REMORAS

I've focused on jobs within the insurance industry, but really, we're talking about an ecosystem here. A species of fish called remoras come to mind, which feeds off the scraps left by sharks as they eat. The failures of self-reform have created inefficiencies that can feed a school of people living in the wake of insurance companies as they swim.

We've created so much distrust between insurers and employers, complicated by a world of choices so expensive and so convoluted for employers, that they turn to brokers to negotiate on their behalf and explain their options for covering employees—brokers who are regulated to greater or lesser extents in different states and whose own relationships with insurance companies may involve incentives that employers don't know exist. There is no question brokers and consultants are needed in this industry; someone has to make sense of the chaos for the buyer. But we have to ask why it's so chaotic to begin with.

We've created armies of pharmaceutical sales reps, whose ability to influence physicians impacts the drugs they prescribe for you, while at the same time, pharmaceutical marketers fill your TV, magazines, and social media feed with ads intended to encourage you to ask for their drugs above other treatments. It's not science that drives these critical choices; it's sales.

We've made it so difficult for patients to get from Point A to Point B in terms of managing their own care that we've made way for care navigators who work for health systems that want to keep you in their costly centers, or navigators who work for payers that want to steer you to the lowest cost, regardless of quality.

There are many good people filling these roles, and in many cases, they do really good work. But the truth is there's nothing essential about the roles themselves. They exist because of a flawed and inefficient system.

CONFLICTS OF INTEREST

We've all heard people talk about healthcare's systemic issues. I think the meaning behind those words is that the people who set the rules, pay for care, and deliver care all have entangled interests and incentives that leave them unwilling to actually change a thing. At the end of the day, health insurance organizations are making billions and billions of dollars off of the status quo. It ain't broke for them—so why would they want to fix it?

The financial and housing crisis of 2008 gave rise to the concept of "too big to fail." Certain private institutions were so central to our economic well-being that they simply could not be allowed to go out of business, no matter what.

Apply that concept to healthcare, and you'll see that the stakes could not be higher. Instead of losing millions of homes to foreclosure, we're talking potentially about losing millions of lives. Instead of losing billions from the economy, we're talking trillions.

Talk about a sector that's truly too big to fail, and we're talking about healthcare. We've *all* got entangled interests in it.

Hank Paulson, the secretary of the treasury during the 2008 housing crisis, put it this way: "Complexity is the enemy of transparency, and complexity is bad in finance." Well, complexity is bad in healthcare too.

Let's look at just some of these interests and how they're holding us back.

POLITICIANS VS. EMPLOYERS

Healthcare is local. Recall that your zip code is a better predictor of your health status than your genetics. And the politicians entrusted with making the decisions that most affect healthcare at the local level are local too—the mayor, governor, state senators or representatives. Not only do they have control or influence over some of the largest local municipalities and unions, they often decide how government plans are administered locally, how insurance companies are regulated, how hospitals are regulated, how access to care and affordability are regulated.

At the same time, these politicians are always going to be influenced by their constituents, and foremost among them are the largest employers in the area. They provide the jobs that keep voters happy and the contributions that fill reelection campaign accounts.

Who is the largest employer at the state, regional, or local level? Oftentimes, it's a hospital, a healthcare system, or an insurance company. If it's not, then it's probably Walmart, but even then, rest assured that right behind them in the top five, you'll find your local healthcare provider and insurer. Yikes—it's the very organizations that are profiting from the existing system.

If the insurance company is doing well and the hospital is doing well, they have every reason to influence the politicians to keep things just the way they are. And the politicians have every reason to listen. Again, I'm not calling out anyone specifically here—I'm just describing the nature of the forces at work.

LARGEST CLIENT VS. INSURANCE COMPANY

The most profitable line of business for almost every insurance company is their commercial line of business—their employer-sponsored coverage, preferably on a fully insured product with everything carved in. For the employer, it's a cost of doing business so significant that studies have shown it's holding wages down. For the employee, it's a significant chunk of their pre- and post-tax paycheck. For the insurance company, it's essentially a requirement for profits.

Now, in many markets, who are the biggest employers? The biggest buyer of health insurance? Here's a hint: I mentioned them before because they have a unique influence on local politics.

The hospitals and their healthcare systems.

Some have become health insurance companies too—IDFS, where the payer and the provider are combined into one broader entity.

But the vast majority of the time, that's not the case. So what you have is the major healthcare provider buying health insurance from a carrier angling for their business. Even though it's a regulated sport, there is a lot that is up for negotiation.

How can an insurance company be true to its fiduciary responsibility to its beneficiaries when the entity it's negotiating with is its biggest commercial client? How can you do it?

Here's a simplistic example: an insurance carrier comes to a health system, its largest employer in a given region, and tells them they need to increase their premium, or administrative rates 2 to 3 percent year over year. What's the healthcare system going to say? Well, the way we make money is from insurance reimbursement, so we need to increase our reimbursement rates, and if it's not through you, it's going to have to be through another carrier.

If this isn't the most bizarre form of passing the buck, then I don't know what is.

Here's where it lands: you shine my shoe; I'll shine yours. You raise your premium rates; I increase my reimbursement rates. A first-year college student in Econ 101 could tell something's wrong in that dynamic. The insurance company is supposed to drive the hard bargain to keep rates affordable, but the company and the hospital system both need each other to be profitable. Who often gets stuck with the outcome of that entangled relationship?

The local employers and their workers, who are outside that equation.

INSURANCE COMPANY VS. PHARMACEUTICAL REBATE

When an insurance company decides what drugs to

cover—its formulary—it naturally goes toward the drug manufacturers and Pharmaceutical Benefits Managers (PBMs) that provide them the highest-efficacy, lowest-cost drug. Beneficiaries, as they go to get their drugs, want to see the lower prices.

Enter the pharmaceutical rebate. These rebates are based on unique calculations that essentially tie back to the volume of a specific pharmaceutical filled—and the rebate is typically paid to the insurance company.

Some states and brokers have picked up on these rebates and require that they be passed back entirely to the employer, 100 percent. They want the employer who's paying the bill to benefit from the savings. But that's not the case in many places.

The result gives the proverbial middleman—the insurance company—an incentive to align its formulary with drug manufacturers and PBMs that pay a higher rebate. We're not talking about pennies here. We're talking about millions and millions of dollars flowing to insurance companies because they're willing to cover this drug but not that one. This undermentioned area of the market comes with a healthy margin and often leads to insurers developing or partnering to develop their own PBMs.

Once, again, there is nothing illegal in this. But if you knew your local oil-change shop was getting paid a rebate to use one type of oil over another, at the very least, you'd want to know, and at the most, you'd ask for quality standards, transparency, and a discounted oil rate to account for their rebate.

PATIENT ADVOCACY GROUPS VS. INSURANCE COMPANIES

Lest you think insurance companies and big health systems are always the beneficiaries of conflicts of interest, that is certainly not the case. Consider **patient advocacy groups**.

As I've said, the commercial line of business is often the most lucrative line of business, not only for the insurance carrier but the healthcare providers. If the health system gets paid one hundred dollars for a procedure on Medicare, they might get two to five to even ten times the reimbursement rate from a commercial carrier. Rates are often described as multiples of Medicare, and they can be extremely high. That's especially true if the provider is the only option in a given geography, giving them leverage over the insurer.

Now, if you're a healthcare provider, do you want to provide care to the Medicare patient or the commercial patient? It's the exact same procedure, but often one is going to pay you more than the other.

The world of dialysis for patients with end-stage renal disease—failed kidneys—is dominated by two companies that own about 80 percent of the market. This is big business; as I noted at the beginning of the book, there are more dialysis centers in the United States than there are Taco Bells. I'm talking big! Dialysis is typically administered three times a week for three to four hours every time, and the cost for a patient on a commercial insurance plan is typically between $100,000 and $150,000 a year.

And you have two publicly traded companies that own 80 percent of the market, often relying on commercial insurance to make a profit.

It is extremely difficult to run their business just on government-sponsored patients. There's simply not enough revenue to cover the costs. These companies are also publicly traded, which means they have to report their earnings to the Street. Maximizing profits is their responsibility to their shareholders.

Together, these two companies provided most of the funding for a patient advocacy group dedicated to helping dialysis patients pay their commercial insurance premiums and their costs of treatment, helping to keep them on the higher reimbursement, commercial plan. And according to a report in the *New York Times*, a whistleblower, and a lawsuit, the advocacy group steered its aid to the patients of the two companies.

If that patient lost their commercial coverage due to unemployment, they could qualify for coverage under Medicare immediately, regardless of their age. Alternatively, once they've been on dialysis for thirty-three months, they become eligible for Medicare regardless of employment. By helping patients stay on their commercial insurance for as long as possible, the advocacy group helped two big donors maintain their most profitable line of business.

CONFRONTING CONFLICTS

I'm not trying to be a whistleblower myself here. Everything I've stated above is publicly known and well documented. The vast majority of people working across these businesses aren't ill-willed. They don't wake up in the morning looking forward to screwing someone else over. My point is that good people are working in a system with a bunch of incentives that drive them in directions that don't serve the collective "us" well.

The shortcomings I've described in the insurance industry's self-reform efforts notwithstanding, I actually still keep the faith with insurance companies. Their primary business interest is more aligned with the individual than the health system. Yup, I said it! Insurers will enjoy a higher profit profile off a relatively healthy population than would a health system.

The issue is the conflicts that riddle our current system. We need to acknowledge and own them. We need to take an honest look at the relationships we've permitted and what governs each influence economically, then ask the question: Is this exactly what we want?

I think we'll agree on the answer.

WHERE TO?

If you didn't get riled up as you've read to this point, then I'm not doing my job.

In Part 1, we looked at the poles of opinion that dominate the political debate over healthcare and how neither the free-market nor a government-dependent system can deliver the low-cost, high-quality care we seek. In Part 2, we've examined the shortcomings of the insurance industry's efforts to self-reform. I could cite many more examples, but I believe the point is clear: the sector has too much inertia going in the wrong direction.

The sum of these two parts is intolerable. Lives are at stake. Health insurance costs inhibit wage growth, and peer-reviewed studies continue to show that medical expenses were responsible for more than 60 percent of personal bankruptcies in our country in the past decade. You can contest the figure, but the fact is we're paying too much for what we actually get.

It's unconscionable to walk away from these realities.

So the question is: Where should we go next?

PART 3

STARTING OVER

CHAPTER 9

ACKNOWLEDGING OUR HEALTHCARE REALITIES

I hope by now I've made the shortcomings of our "perfect" failure of a healthcare system clear. But I also think in exploring it, we've identified some inescapable realities of healthcare in America that any viable solution must reflect in order to win support and deliver on the twin goals of better outcomes at lower costs.

I think of the list that follows as acknowledgments—recognitions of reality whose implications point us in the direction of workable change.

Here are my ideas:

1. Healthcare spending is our country's "thing," and it will

always dominate a large percentage of the American economy.

2. There will always be a government role in healthcare.
3. It's not and it can't be a purely free market.
4. But free markets do drive progress.
5. The system is too big to reform through iteration.
6. The industry is filled with good people and good intentions.
7. We already know how to deliver better healthcare outcomes.
8. Incentives drive behavior.
9. Limited resources mean constraints, and constraints mean there will be losers.
10. The winners in the current system sit on top, so the impetus for change must come from below.

Let's step through each of these in more detail.

1. HEALTHCARE SPENDING IS OUR THING.

The healthcare economy is at the heart of our society. It is the twenty-first-century path to a solid career. We support millions of Americans with jobs in healthcare, amounting to roughly 14 percent of the working economy. More than 18 percent of the gross domestic product is tied to healthcare-related spending.

At the end of the day, those people need jobs. There are

too many people who went to nursing school, who went to medical school, who hold their master's degrees in public health and healthcare administration. There are millions of people who went to vocational programs to learn how to be a surgical technician, an EHR specialist, a medical assistant, and many more. And there are even more people employed by the supportive infrastructure and supply chain that are required for delivering care. We can't magically tell them their certifications, degrees, and extensive training are not valued anymore and they're going to be unemployed.

So acknowledgment number one is that healthcare and its related spending is our country's thing. It's always going to dominate a large percentage of our economy. Anything otherwise would be catastrophic. That's not to say we can't require better outcomes for that spending, truly pushing to get more for our dollar, or squeezing out the jobs that exist only because of the system's inefficiencies.

But the spending will be there going forward. It's fundamental to our economy.

2. THERE WILL ALWAYS BE A GOVERNMENT ROLE IN HEALTHCARE.

In 2021, there are more than 100 million Americans on government-sponsored healthcare programs. That's nearly one-third of our population. I'm not saying that's the right proportion. I'm saying that's reality. There will always be gradations in society and therefore always be a group of people who are less fortunate. There will always be children without access to health coverage and veterans who expect the government to protect them. Simply put, there will always be a need for a government safety net.

In addition, there will always be a need for regulations to establish guardrails that protect the interests of the public. This is not to say that the government should be driving the show. I don't believe it should or even can. But centralized governing bodies will always be involved, as the incentives drive behavior that does not always align with the broader good.

The government should establish the minimum level of care that every American can expect, ensure that those without means receive it, and that the players in the health-care industry deliver it. I want to stress this, though: when I say minimum, I mean it. I do not believe people on a government-sponsored program should get better benefits than those who aren't.

For me, as always, it's a matter of math, not ideology. Any person who's working and paying taxes is fueling this healthcare economic machine. As we've discussed, the commercial beneficiary is an essential ingredient for health plans and providers. These people should be protected—

and also incentivized to continue creating value through access to equal if not better care. After all, they're the ones generating the tax dollars and premiums to support the government-sponsored care for the unfortunate, just as they're the ones creating the most profitable segment for payers and providers.

Perhaps this position invites a counterargument: this idea will only continue to perpetuate inequity within our society. Inequity is different from inequality. I believe inequity needs to be solved, as I've argued throughout this book. But that doesn't mean that we can't set a minimum level of care to ensure equity while also creating differentiated experiences for others. The belief in a better life drives people to work every day. We often express it as the belief that you can get ahead. So, ahead of what? The average. It's a dynamic of self-propulsion that drives our economy as people push our country's average upward.

This is what actually delineates universal health coverage from socialized medicine. Socialized medicine refers to everyone getting the same thing. I am not a proponent of this because of the critical incentives it removes. Universal health coverage, on the other hand, ensures that everyone has access to a minimum standard of coverage and care— and I am all for it!

The government must ensure that the rights of society's

most needy are respected and their needs met. But it also must remember who it's being funded by to begin with. The appropriate government role in healthcare is clear to me: provide a safety net for a select group and serve as a regulating body that's needed in a high-stakes sector. It shouldn't be the long-term answer for everyone.

3. IT'S NOT AND IT CAN'T BE A PURELY FREE MARKET.

I want to make this clear: I believe that free markets are better than regulated markets in almost any sector. But we need to acknowledge that healthcare isn't and can't be a truly free market. People are in no position to act as a true consumer; they cannot make the informed decisions essential to such a market. They don't understand the medical market. They don't understand the implications of their choices. They don't understand their needs. They don't understand the pricing or costs. When people can't easily ascertain the value in the choices they face, a regulated market is the better solution.

Even if we were to correct the litany of obstacles that preclude the healthcare market from operating freely, I still fear that the average American would not act in their own best interest. I know it's easier to say, "Screw it then, that's their own fault." And this is not me turning into Big Brother, but rather just me looking at the facts. Here's an example:

the majority of Americans are overweight, meaning they have selected to increase their health risk. In a free market, we'd let these tragic decisions have tragic outcomes—and many more people would die, as there would be no reason to insure them or try to manage their care. Insulin would be priced to the moon due to the demand. So either you heavily regulate the industry (to control prices), or you try to change the behavior of the patients (to control demand); in either direction, you're left holding a paternalistic stick, and far from a free market.

4. BUT FREE MARKETS DO DRIVE PROGRESS.

I want to make this clear too: competition is an essential element of any sector of our economy, including healthcare. It drives evolution, it generates growth, and it carries the system forward.

While the healthcare market must be regulated, it must also be allowed to thrive. The system won't sustain itself if it sucks the life out of healthcare businesses. These businesses create jobs and value.

Are points three and four contradictory? I don't think so.

I don't need a Lamborghini. I know its price, I know its value, and no one can force me to buy one. That's a free market. But if someone could force me to spend $350,000 on a Lamborghini without me knowing it, then I'd want that market to be regulated so that I, the consumer, was protected. I'm cool with Lamborghinis; they raise the bar for every other carmaker out there—and if every manufacturer is chasing the profits that come with building better cars, I'll benefit along with them (without buying a Lamborghini, in case you were wondering).

5. THE SYSTEM IS TOO BIG TO REFORM THROUGH ITERATION.

American healthcare suffers from systemic issues, and for decades now, we've been attempting to address them through point-based reforms. It's like squeezing a balloon: the air just moves to a new area. We're not going to retrofit our way to a solution, and we're not going to iterate our way there either. Systemic issues require systemic solutions. American healthcare is simply too big and convoluted to tweak our way forward.

It's also worth noting that so many wonderful healthcare ideas die due to inadequate scale. Especially in health insurance, where critical mass is just that: critical. We've seen this play out time and time again, most recently with the demise of Haven—the joint venture by Amazon, J.P. Morgan, and Berkshire Hathaway that intended to lower healthcare costs and improve quality for their combined one million employees. It closed in 2020 after only three years, with many pointing to inadequate scale as the reason for its downfall.

The problem isn't the air inside the balloon; it's the balloon. We're going to need to pop it.

6. THE INDUSTRY IS FILLED WITH GOOD PEOPLE AND GOOD INTENTIONS.

Once again, I'm not pointing the finger at malicious intent. Very few people are deliberately and methodically profiteering and driving the American healthcare system into the ground. The people who are actually delivering care aren't involved in negotiating the prices. They want to do the right thing and help the patient. No insurance manager charged with developing a preventive care program wants it to fail or is trying to screw an employer client.

The good news in this is that the culture at the heart of American healthcare is strong. The culture of care is not the problem.

The problem is that 99 percent of the people in the system can't see or understand the system as a whole. Even middle to upper management, the people who lead different divisions at major healthcare players, doesn't realize just how bad or avoidable many issues within the system are. Their unknowing ignorance brings bliss.

It's a world of silos, and no one who's stuck in a silo can truly see and understand the whole landscape.

7. WE ALREADY KNOW HOW TO DELIVER BETTER HEALTHCARE OUTCOMES.

Population health management programs work; chronic disease prevention and management programs work—if they're adequately resourced and given time. But in our current healthcare economy, they're not viable because they don't always deliver a quick enough return on the investment required to justify them.

We have efficacious programs focused on the right things. But they won't survive long enough to make a difference until we alter and stabilize the financial vehicle on which they ride.

It's not as if the healthcare sector is a cancer for which we have no treatment or cure. We know what programs work from an impact perspective. As interventions, they work. As financial propositions, they don't—yet.

8. INCENTIVES DRIVE BEHAVIOR.

What you measure, you get, and what you reward, you *really* get. That's called upside risk. Impose penalties instead of rewards, and you'll get less instead of more. That's called downside risk.

The healthcare system is governed by incentives—and the story of its shortcomings boils down to this: perverse incentives drive bad outcomes.

But if you can reposition and simplify the incentives and disincentives, you can drive significant behavior change in the right direction.

9. LIMITED RESOURCES MEAN CONSTRAINTS, AND CONSTRAINTS MEAN THERE WILL BE LOSERS.

Here's a truth that most people in the system or those who want to change it don't recognize: at the end of the day, we're talking about money, and the supply of money isn't endless. We can't continue to pay for programs that produce no better outcomes than cheaper programs in other countries.

We need to acknowledge that we're working with limited resources—and that means there will be losers in any solution we develop.

I recognize the counterargument here too: price is not inevitable, it's set by humans, and if we control it, then we can increase affordability. I believe that approach amounts to a gateway drug to socialized medicine. If the market doesn't govern or at least influence price, that's what you're headed for. You run the risk of going so far that the innovation and transformation our country continuously yearns for may not be adequately rewarded.

There will be people who lose jobs, who either can't or won't learn the new skills they need to make a meaningful contribution. There will be sectors of the healthcare system that are deemed to add no value. There will be treatments that, due to their one in a thousand chance of working, will be priced too high for many to afford. These are realities we need to recognize and address. We need to be unafraid to ask hard questions and to make hard decisions.

When it comes to evolving our workforce, I'd rather be responsible for firing someone than killing someone else by perpetuating a system that delivers inadequate healthcare—simple as that!

10. THE WINNERS IN THE CURRENT SYSTEM SIT ON TOP, SO THE IMPETUS FOR CHANGE MUST COME FROM BELOW.

The people and forces that govern this current system benefit from the status quo. Healthcare providers and insurance carriers are likely among the biggest employers in your state, and the politician who pays attention to them isn't typically going to leap into the vanguard of meaningful change. Neither are the executives who lead those organizations and answer to their boards and shareholders.

These are the very people who hold the power. So the pressure for change needs to be supported by them but most likely should come from somewhere else—from a nontraditional source.

If you're wondering what I mean by that, bear with me. I may be talking about you. But first, let's begin the conversation about what change built on the realities I've just outlined might look like.

CHAPTER 10

THE NEXT CHAPTER IN HEALTHCARE IS A NEW BOOK

You've heard it before. It's time to turn a new page. It's time to write a new chapter. But when it comes to American healthcare, turning new pages and writing new chapters won't be nearly enough.

We need to write a new book. We need to leave the past behind and start again, building a new healthcare system that better meets our needs. We have to build from the ground up, starting with a new foundation.

I can't wish away the political realities that stand in the way of such fundamental reform. But given all that's at stake, I'm unwilling to accept anything less than this goal. I believe that once I've laid out my case, you'll agree.

I can't write the entire solution, the whole book, in one chapter either. It's going to take the work of many minds balancing many interests. But I can begin to articulate the outline, reimagining how we better insure the health of Americans and deliver on the goals I've described from the beginning: high-quality outcomes at an affordable cost delivered through a humanized experience built for a real world in which people usually make the easiest and not necessarily the best choice.

What are the core elements of a solution? The levers we need to pull in order to set meaningful change in motion? Here's where I'd begin:

1. Individualized commercial insurance
2. Payer-agnostic platforms
3. Local governance
4. For patients, a modernized experience
5. For providers, a focus on care
6. For administrators, cross-industry pollination
7. For employees, a modernized skillset
8. For the needy, federalized government support programs
9. All complemented by a bimodal approach

Let's take a look at each of these in turn.

1. INDIVIDUALIZED COMMERCIAL INSURANCE

I believe we made a wrong turn as we came out of World War II, when we put the burden of providing health insurance on employers. I'm not suggesting that the prevailing option of national healthcare, which other countries chose, was any better. What I lament is the missed opportunity to take full advantage of a moment when the political window for holistic change was wide open. We need to return to that moment of original sin, and this is where I'd start: by making the decision about which insurance to buy an individual's decision, not the employer's.

The single largest block of insured Americans—180 million people—are covered by employer-sponsored plans. But as costs have risen, the burden of meeting them has shifted to employees, either directly through premiums and high deductibles or indirectly through suppressed wages. At the same time, the quality of many of these plans has deteriorated, leaving those they cover a false sense of insurance. This will only get worse as a higher percentage of Americans age into Medicare coverage, forcing providers to squeeze more money from the declining percentage of the commercially insured population.

Sure, they're "covered." But the out-of-pocket expenses they're responsible for are so high relative to their income and savings that they're functionally underinsured. I've talked about the figures before: a typical high-deductible health plan for an average-sized family will bring a $12,000 out-of-pocket requirement, and that's high enough to wipe out over 50 percent of American families' total savings.

They also have a false sense of choice. The most important decisions aren't made by the employees but by their Human Relations department or their C-suite. As I mentioned earlier, by the time the employee chooses, there have been (from what I can count) at least seventy-five choices made by insurance executives, regulators, brokers, and the company's leadership before the employee gets to "choose" the coverage option that works best. As we've discussed, depending on the size of the employer, these choices are typically governed by insurance brokers who, no matter how good their intentions, can have incentives to peddle one plan over another that aren't necessarily visible to the employer.

Most employees are also unaware of the effect on their paycheck. The second-largest line item in the expense budget for almost any employer is the health insurance benefit. The employer's need to pay that bill is being subsidized by holding down wage growth or shifting more of the cost share to the employee. As the cost of healthcare continues to grow, that burden will grow with it.

At the same time, because costs are still rising and employer-sponsored plans still cover a large percentage of the total cost of care, employees are stripped of their incentive to shop for care. The plans are hopelessly convoluted, but even so, if 90 percent of your cost is covered, why shop? The incentive to shop—and to compete for business—is a core element of a free market.

How does ending employer-sponsored insurance help?

It would require insurance carriers to compete for business at the individual level in the same way that many of them compete for the vast majority of Medicare Advantage customers and Affordable Care Act (Obamacare) individual products. This competition takes place in a regulated state-level marketplace, which helps protect consumers while insurers vie for their business.

This would also free us from the uniquely incentivized world of employer health benefits, where an employer's choices are often filtered through a broker, leaving carriers as dependent on fostering personal relationships with brokers as they are on the objective pricing or underwriting principles associated with their insurance quote. Brokers would still have an important role to play, but it would be based on utility and driven by competition, as the best brokers compete for an individual's business. I'm sure the inevitable Yelp reviews would help evolve this industry too.

Individualizing the process would also create a demand

for transparent health insurance pricing structures. Think about the competition for auto insurance: it has modernized the experience and product options. It's a critical ingredient in fostering the affordability that we're after.

2. PAYER-AGNOSTIC PLATFORMS

We are beset by the complexity that arises from the different processes and requirements that each insurer creates for its own products. It's an administrative nightmare that fosters inefficiencies and confusion. As insurers continue to "differentiate" themselves, they continue to grow what I call the integration divide between providers and patients—meaning it's harder to deliver coordinated, more efficient, and more effective care. Nearly everyone loses because of this approach, including the insurers.

I believe a better alternative is a singular, state-specific platform serving community needs that every insurer that does business in the state must support. The amount of financial support from each insurer would be proportionate to their respective percentage of total revenue within the state. The formula could use a blended methodology, weighting different lines of business differently to support and protect lower-margin, government-specific insurers.

POPULATION HEALTH MANAGEMENT

I see payer-agnostic platforms as the key to delivering on the promise of Population Health Management (PHM) by addressing not just the symptoms of diabetes or substance abuse, say, but the underlying Social Determinants of Health (SDOH): local issues such as education, housing, and jobs.

I've talked about how initiatives such as diabetes prevention programs have been shown to work in terms of health but fail financially because the return on investment for the insurer is so long in coming that they typically won't receive the full financial benefit. A payer-agnostic platform removes that obstacle because every insurer in the state it serves shares in supporting it. They'd share in governing it too, along with community and state representatives.

PHM programs work. They're effective. I think the primary reason they do not see broad success is that the financial numbers usually don't work as the insurer needs them to. Under this approach, they will.

The centralized platform can also make individual health records readily accessible to providers across different institutions. Such **Health Information Exchanges** (HIEs) have been shown to be extremely effective in states that fully buy in, requiring all stakeholders to participate. These centralized databases for clinical information enable a provider now treating a patient in one hospital to have access to imaging taken at another. HIEs also are essential for assessing trends across a population, allowing epidemiologists, say, to look at the level of COVID-19 positive tests at the county level across a state to inform decisions about quarantines and reopening businesses.

It's not a novel concept. But it's not universally applied—payer-agnostic platforms can supercharge the value realized through PHM programs.

CONSUMER INSIGHTS

When you shop in the grocery store, you'll find a nutrition information panel on the side of every food item you buy. You can compare calories, saturated fat, and more.

A common platform creates the same opportunity in healthcare. That's central to informed consumer choice, and it's nearly impossible right now. A doctor may be a tier-one preferred provider in one insurer's high-value network, be a tier-two provider in another, and not even be included in the network of a third. It's the same doctor practicing the same medicine, and three different insurance companies are giving you different assessments based on their definitions around quality and cost of care.

This common set of insights must also be easily accessible.

Almost everyone understands miles per gallon. When you buy a car, you don't need to know how an engine works or the mechanics of fuel consumption; you just need to know that you prefer a car that gets twenty-five miles per gallon and not ten. I do not believe that healthcare is so inherently complicated that we can't make it simple for a layman. The issue is that right now, few have an incentive to try.

These insights would also support the "shopability" needed for an individualized commercial insurance approach, as more people take on more risk for their own decision-making.

SIMPLIFIED ADMINISTRATION

Credentialing a provider as in-network is a long and involved process that can take anywhere from two to six months or longer. The provider, mind you, has already been licensed to practice medicine; this is simply credentialing them to be within the insurer's network. This process is fairly consistent among insurance providers. And yet the provider has to go through it one by one, providing what's largely the same information in a process that's—to use a polite, understated word—archaic.

A single centralized, crowd-sourced platform changes that dynamic. It would create one centralized ledger where every provider lists their billing address, their telephone number, their fax number, all of their board certifications—every single thing that's needed in order to credential them. Entered once, in one location, easy to update, and accessible to every payer for credentialing purposes.

This serves other purposes too. Medicare currently conducts massive audits of public-facing provider directories, where insurers are required to list their networks with provider directory information such as contact particulars and office locations. Stakes are high; fines can be as large as $25,000 per Medicare patient. A doctor who moves an office, develops a partnership, decides to work for a larger health system, or maybe even decides not to accept new patients, has to communicate that back to each insurer, which in turn needs to validate that information and make it publicly available.

PLATFORM POWER

My belief is that supporting all of these components—Population Health Management programs, clinical insights, and simplified administration, all delivered through payer-agnostic platforms—should be table stakes for carriers that want to compete for business in a given state. They are too important to limit to a "differentiated value" that a consumer can only access if they're lucky enough for everyone above them in the decision-making process to choose the right payer partner.

3. LOCAL GOVERNANCE

Decisions about removing employer-sponsored insurance and creating payer-agnostic platforms require a governing body to make them happen. This should be done at the state, not the federal level. I'm not trying to pick a political side in saying this. You need a level of governance that's high enough to encompass all the different players but localized enough to make decisions based on a particular region's needs and realities. A one-size-fits-all approach at the federal level won't work in this instance.

We've seen the federal CMS (the Centers for Medicare and Medicaid Services) approach this challenge in different ways. In the end, they've built a lot of flexibility into the regulations they issue to enable governance at the local level. Reimbursement levels for Medicare Advantage vary not just from state to state but from county to county.

If it were up to me, government officials would play a measured role in this governing body; I'd prefer to see a hybrid of public and private stakeholders similar to Medicare Advantage, which has shown that the public-private partnership can work. Their role would be significant, and they'd be vested with real authority.

BENCHMARKING

In a number of states now, we're seeing governing bodies

set cost growth benchmarks—a rate of increase in costs that insurers and their affiliated stakeholder can't surpass in a given year. Massachusetts provides a clear example: in 2019, they set a benchmark of 3.1 percent.

The problem is that they haven't shown their teeth yet. At the end of the year, growth came in at 3.6 percent, but none of the institutions that drove the benchmark above the target faced serious repercussions.

It's not because hospitals don't want to do the right thing; it's because they can't get out of their own way. Insurance companies don't know how to help them transform, and even if they did, they represent a proportion of the total business of the provider's patient panel. Along with the power to enforce consequences, the governing body would carry the responsibility of helping them create a path toward success through tested and proven best practices.

Such best-practice benchmarking could be achieved through defining evidence-based disease pathways for well-known chronic diseases: diabetes, COPD, CHF, etc. The pathways would describe the sequence of appropriate interventions, where and how they should be delivered, who should deliver them, and the expected costs, while making all this information publicly available. This will provide the plausibility test that is also often missing from these cost targets—a realistic path to achieving the goal.

Finally, the governing body would play a role in directing how commercial insurance profit margins are invested. I can hear the response now: "Whoa! What? Why?"

First, a government role in the distribution of health insurance profits is not a novel concept. When Obamacare's public exchange was rolled out, the agreement in essence was that if one payer made more money on a product than another payer, they'd have to share their risk-adjusted profits.

Second, when an insurance company decides to innovate by improving its internal operations, that will theoretically boost its profit margin. If the company is not going to pass its profit margin improvements to the individual or the employer in the form of lower premiums, I don't believe we should prioritize that—not given how much remains to be done in improving on clinical care outcomes that are, quite frankly, abysmal for a highly developed country such as ours.

Let's say the dominant insurer in your market makes a profit of $100 million in the same year that your spouse dies of detectable, avoidable cancer and then announces that it's investing in an artificial intelligence platform for its claims processing unit. Wouldn't you say, "Wait. Couldn't you take the money that we all pay you and invest it in cancer research instead?"

If you don't agree, fine. But if you do, shouldn't we peel this one back, open our minds, and consider a different approach?

At the end of the day, we're all paying for healthcare and the profits it generates. It only makes sense to put some sort of regulation on top and ensure the proceeds are being allocated responsibly. That's especially the case when the organizations involved are not-for-profit, which means they're essentially a community asset, free from most taxation, when at the same time, they're often behaving like for-profit players.

4. MODERNIZED PATIENT EXPERIENCE

When it comes to healthcare, the modern patient has nothing like a modernized experience. Go to one provider, and you're handed a pen and a piece of paper on a clipboard. Go to another, and they're using an iPad. Go to a third, and everything's virtual.

The fact that we haven't standardized this is wild. The next frontier of healthcare delivery is digital health. If we leave it up to healthcare providers alone, we're going to foster one more disparate, inefficient system where everyone has their own chat rooms and means of engagement. Healthcare providers are not product developers, which means they've chosen to cobble together a number of point-specific solutions to enable "digital front door" strategies. These strategies are highly dependent on third-party software companies that have their own profit margin needs and aspirations of financial growth, adding another margin-focused stakeholder to the healthcare cost equation. What's more, inconsistency in access and experience is going to marginalize more people who shouldn't be marginalized.

What would a modernized patient experience look like?

In the immediate future, it's most likely mobile-first in nature. You can access it and engage with it on your phone. We're all on our phones; that may be the one thing we have in common right now.

It provides palatable, graspable, accessible insights to inform patient decisions around price and quality of care. If we don't have a modernized experience, we can't have a shoppable experience.

It doesn't always require a new download. One of the biggest problems we have is that every insurance carrier and healthcare provider has their own app. This usually feeds into some "omni-channel strategy," ostensibly enabling patients to connect by text or email or video chat. But everyone's channel is different, so we're not really solving problems. We're simply trading them.

Perhaps addressing this is the realm of the governing body too. Who better to answer what should be a collective question: What portal are all of us going to use to communicate?

CARE PLANNING

A truly modernized experience isn't limited to technology. Supporting this modernized engagement strategy, we also need to modernize our approach to things like care planning.

I'd propose requiring advanced directives and an appointed healthcare agent for every person as part of the insurance application process. The choices are entirely the patient's to make. Not everyone wants to be intubated, to be left unable to communicate with anybody, to live their life in a vegetative state. I would not require anyone to sign a Do Not Resuscitate (DNR) order. What you *are* required to do would be to state your choice. It's a difficult topic to raise, and providers suffer from a terrible lack of training in how to do it. But we need to talk about it because not doing so will continue to drive significant costs for the system as a whole, whether the person whose life is being prolonged wants it or not. This fact is only exacerbated by an aging population.

Some quick back-of-the-napkin math tells me that if just 5 percent more of our country's terminally ill population selected a DNR, then we could save in excess of $50 billion. This is a high-cost bucket, and we just don't want to talk about it. It's become a "death panel" taboo topic. Unfortunately, this has downstream impacts on everyone paying into the system, and with an aging population, we must make an honest conversation about this part of the modernized patient experience too. Almost every other country addresses it in some proactive form. We're afraid to, and that needs to change.

FINANCIAL INCENTIVES

Finally, a modernized patient experience features financial incentives to drive behavior change. A company called Wellth has shown how effective this can be by using loss aversion to incentivize patient behavior change.

Take adhering to your drug protocol, for example. The issue is typically that patients don't take their medicines as prescribed. They have a hard time regulating their own health.

Wellth creates an incentive to take that prescription by prospectively providing a patient a monthly amount of money, and then penalizing the patient a percentage of that money every time they don't adhere. Seem cruel? Well, negative incentives—loss aversion—have been shown to be twice as effective as positive incentives that require change before the reward.

How could someone possibly know if I've taken my prescription? One way is simply to require you to take a photo of the pill in your hand with your phone. Some manufacturers have the ability to embed sensors within the pill itself, telling your phone (and the cloud) when it's been swallowed. Taking your weight each day could work the same way: step on the scale, record it via Bluetooth, and get the credit you're due.

I recognize it's another tough topic. We're uncomfortable with financial incentives around patient behavior; regulation typically prevents much of it for fear of inducing or steering patients around what's seen as matters of personal choice.

That type of regulation is outdated, and fortunately, it's slowly changing. It's a form of paternalism that has outlived its time. In almost every other facet of life, financial incentives are in play and to our benefit. I choose a credit card because I get points to use on Amazon. I use a ride-sharing app because I accrue points toward discounts for future rides. I have discount programs to shop at certain stores. Just about every industry has introduced incentivization to drive behavior change.

Let me put this on the table: Why not incentivize organ donations? We have over one hundred thousand people waiting for an organ donation today and millions of people who aren't on the list to donate. People are dying for lack of organ donors. A contentious topic, I know, raising the prospect that it would drive people in financial need to take on larger clinical risk than their wealthier counterparts. But there's moral risk in the status quo too: we're allowing people's uninformed biases regarding organ donations to drive the health outcomes of innocent community members. I think we have a very fragile mindset regarding this topic—too few are willing to think creatively around driving change. At the very least, we should change organ donation from opt-in to opt-out at the federal level.

What about end-of-life care? As Americans, we are collectively guilty of a save-all mentality. When Grandma's sick, we want to do something—no matter how sick she happens to be. And the last six months of a patient's life can cost more than their last seven years combined.

What if, once Grandma (an FFS Medicare beneficiary) was diagnosed as terminally ill, we put $50,000 in a bank account for the family, with no access to it until she dies? For every day that certain high-cost interventions are used to keep her alive, interventions that are not supported by evidence or efficacy, we'd subsidize the cost of her care by first applying the $50,000. Grandma's ninety years old, she's lived a good life, and the end is at hand. How would that financial incentive impact the decisions that her family is making for her?

Uncomfortable? Yes. Unethical? I don't think so. Health-care is a precious resource. When the death of a loved one is inescapable, we have a shared interest in fostering not just a family's emotional but also rational decision-making in response. By keeping your Medicare-covered spouse alive for one more day in the ICU at the age of ninety, you are taking resources that could be used for the Medicare-covered sixty-five-year-old who was just diagnosed with ESRD. We have to consider the fungibility of our spending in healthcare and how to regulate such a finite resource, especially if it's being paid by the government.

We've enabled a system that prioritizes individual choice over all else. Why? It's not the individual who's paying for the consequences. This is an instance where big-government funding and a small-government mentality don't mesh. We're living in a have-it-both-ways gray space.

5. A FOCUS ON CARE

Here's a new normal for you: if you are a credentialed healthcare provider, you *must* practice medicine 85 percent of the time you have agreed to work. If you are full time, 85 percent of that time. If you work part time, 85 percent of that time.

Why is that a foundational element of a new system? First, because there's a massive provider shortage in America. Second, because providers will tell you that they're currently spending 40 to 50 percent of their time on administrative tasks—work that can either be automated, delegated, or removed altogether. That's time that could be spent seeing other patients. Far better for the system's cost structure to address a capacity issue by automating administrative workflows than to train up twice as many providers.

In reality, we'll need some of both: automated or eliminated administrative tasks and training for more providers.

But there's another reason for starting with the 85 percent mandate: provider burnout. The burden of administrative tasks is one of the primary reasons providers cite for being unhappy in their work or, worse yet, stepping away from it—leaving the profession at a time when their experience makes them more valuable than ever.

The mandate isn't actually directed at providers—who I assume would love to abide by it—but at the administrators who are making it impossible for them to do it. It's targeted at the hospital systems and large provider groups and even the insurance companies and saying, "We're telling you that 85 percent of the provider's time is going to be focused on clinical care. Whatever documentation that you need from them needs to be automated, delegated, or completely removed from their clinical workflow."

The answer can't be pushing the administrative work to the advanced practice providers or the nurses either. That's often what happens: the doctor just passes the work down the clinical chain of command.

Establishing this mandate forces a number of stakeholders to think more creatively about where time should be spent and how to make it happen. It will lead to more innovation and optimization with the clinical and administrative workflows. It could even lead to providers shopping prospective employers based upon these merits, further pushing these initiatives ahead as the provider systems compete for talent.

Finally, let's make it transparent. Demonstrate that administrative work is no longer taking up more than 15 percent of the provider's time. And monitor it the same way we do other quality metrics: the Healthcare Effectiveness Data and Information Set (HEDIS), the National Committee for Quality Insurance (NCQA), and more.

I believe this mandate should work in the other direction too. Some of our best doctors are focused on producing academic papers in large academic medical centers. That's fine; I'm all for research. It's essential to the continued evolution of the medical field. But their research should not be counted as clinical care and funded through clinical care budgets. Again, we have a physician shortage in this country, and healthcare is a finite resource; we shouldn't be paying clinicians who are fully licensed and accredited from clinical care budgets if they're not practicing direct care. If a medical center wants to hire a brainiac who doesn't practice writing papers that bring in grant money, great; find another way to fund it.

This paper chase has led to staffing models where residents and fellows do the clinical work of attendings in the interest of facilitating more publications and authorship. Some of our best-trained physicians are barely practicing medicine!

As my friend Raj Shrestha says, "We need a workflow of the future to support the workforce of the future." Free the caregivers to give care. It's what they're there for, it's what they want to do, we don't have enough of them—and it's what we're all paying them for.

6. CROSS-INDUSTRY POLLINATION

How many times have you said something like this to someone? "We need the Uber (insert Netflix, Amazon, Disney, or Ritz Carlton) of healthcare!" Why? Because these service platforms offer a user experience that transcended any historic expectation for their category.

How do you think these products were made? Honestly—ask yourself, what group of individuals would come together to create an Uber? Hmmm. Do you think it was a group of taxi drivers? No? Of course not. They don't have the skill-set for that, and they don't have the mindset for it either. So who then? Perhaps it took tech engineers and product designers, specialists in legal, finance, IT security, marketing and design, customer experience—oh, and finally, some drivers!

When we look at other industries, we see an obvious need for cross-industry skillsets and different ways of thinking. The benefits are so easy to see that it seems essential for success. Yet when it comes to healthcare, many insiders long shared a knee-jerk reaction: "Healthcare isn't anything like your industry. It's more complicated than you realize." Rather than welcoming cross-industry mind-sharing or alternative functional expertise, we erected barriers to them.

In recent years this has begun to shift. We've seen notable senior executives hired from the likes of Disney, Amazon, Uber, and so on. So why haven't we seen healthcare transformation as a result?

I think the issue lies beneath the top brass. I've worked with many cross-industry senior executives, but as you descend the corporate ladder, the numbers decrease quickly. This is where so much of the problem-solving really takes place. It's not the big multimillion-dollar technology platform migration that preoccupies the senior executive, and yet it's the day-to-day work-arounds that need to be thought through and solved with creativity. It's like corrosion in a pipe. You must go deep to repair it.

It's time to intentionally seek out and hire people with disparate backgrounds and skills all the way down to the entry level. We need to standardize how we account for years of experience in other industries. I've seen hiring managers struggle with this in nearly every company where I've worked—except one: Cricket Health, a company led by Arvind Rajan. Arvind was an early HR leader at LinkedIn, and he is one of the best people managers and evaluators of talent that I've ever known. He has a remarkable ability to look beyond résumés to the person beneath, and he does it with purpose, probing for evidence of a candidate's ability to solve complex problems and overcome challenges. He ties seemingly unrelated facts, personality traits, and unique experiences into a coherent understanding that facilitates cross-industry hiring. I firmly believe this skill is teachable. It's essential for all insurance companies to embrace it because the industry desperately needs people with new and different talents and the mindsets they bring. We're not going to get outside our box without them.

7. MODERNIZED SKILLSET

You don't need me to tell you how fast the world is changing. Keeping up with the curve in healthcare—and maybe even getting ahead of it—is going to require a workforce with new skills. This will involve upskilling workers who are willing to adapt along with new types of hires altogether.

What sorts of skills am I talking about? Here's a short list, far from complete, limited to needs I see emerging in the next five years if they're not already present.

Skills in digital modalities such as Zoom or Webex to support the virtual delivery of care. COVID-19 served as a catalyst for telehealth, and we're already seeing the development of subspecialties in telepsychology, teleprimary, and teledermatology. There will be more.

Skills around streaming, or asynchronous, video. Customers no longer open the snail mail they get from their insurance company. Their email inboxes are so crammed that it's easy to miss things. What's next? A sixty-second video or sound bite that gives them the information they need and is available when they have time to listen or watch. Your communication team is going to need the ability to not just write but to get in front of a camera or mic and deliver information.

Skills to address the many social determinants of health that exist outside the facility of care: exercise trainers, employment specialists, social workers. Already, we see players like Unite Us going into markets and working with multiple organizations to deliver what amounts to payer-agnostic care of the sort I've advocated for. This will only continue to grow and evolve.

Skills around identifying the rising health risks of our time and getting in front of them. Many of these are related to social media—YouTube, Facebook, Twitter, Instagram, TikTok—where bad news and fake news spread six times faster than real news. These are entirely new drivers of healthcare issues, especially mental health. Clinical service teams charged with identifying rising risk populations need to develop or hire people with new skills to address a challenge that I can only see becoming more pervasive.

Skills related to nudging people to change behavior. We have seen the start of formalization of things like "nudge units" at the University of Pennsylvania. I believe we will see more as insurance companies look to influence behavior changes as social media networks do—engagement and marketing tactics to influence you into buying this, commenting on that, reading this—all in an effort to get you to change 1 percent every day.

Skills required to move from reactive to proactive responses to the changes I'm describing, capitalizing on the remarkable progress we've made in analytics. We're moving beyond looking back to review what happened and looking forward to predict what's going to happen next. I'm specifically thinking about the clinical actions taken based on predictive analytics, not the analytics themselves. I think we'll see clinical service teams reaching into populations to address problems before they happen, not after.

Skills needed to develop and deliver insurance products adapted to the growing gig economy, customizable at the individual rather than the employer level. This will require increasingly complicated product designs. We'll need to design them well, administer them efficiently, and present them clearly.

Skills around robotics and automation, a huge area involving everything from internal operations to the member and provider experience. We're already seeing health plans cutting their teeth by using vended solutions, but that's not a long-term strategy. We'll see a shift to insourcing, and this is going to require engineers, product managers, and customer experience specialists too. User experience is a form of human-centered design, a science all its own.

Skills related to—believe it or not—the drones that are already beginning to fill the sky and the personal helicopters already in development. We're going to see drones delivering organs from one area to another in a congested city. We'll see drones covering long distances to deliver supplies to rural healthcare facilities. And it's not going to be long before we see people moving from one area to another.

How will health plans pay for this? Price it? Understand and support it?

Skills around empathy. This is a skill that's undervalued now and will become even more essential in the future. There are certain things robots will never do. So many people live in an online world and are losing touch with this skill. Learning how to read someone's feelings and showing that you understand, that you care—it's not a skill, but it's underappreciated, and it needs to be prioritized.

8. FEDERALIZED GOVERNMENT SUPPORT PROGRAMS

I made the point that local governance should be central to healthcare delivery and reform before addressing the federal role for a reason. It's a big shift. Local governance should be central. There is simply far too much involved in determining a community's priorities and needs to reduce it to a national formula.

But that's not to say decisions about who's in need of government assistance and what support they receive should rest solely at the local level. More than 80 percent of the cost of Medicaid is covered by the federal government, and yet we've allowed states to decide how far to extend coverage to the needy. Big-government funding with small-government administration don't often mix well.

Think about the effects of COVID-19 at the local level, as businesses closed and people lost jobs and with that, access to healthcare coverage. In states that chose not to expand Medicaid when given the incentive to do so by Obamacare, the impact on communities is that much greater. Obamacare even went so far as to permit state-level "innovation waivers" that enabled them to take Medicaid money allocated to them and go off and try new models of coverage and care delivery.

When a program is subsidized by the federal government to the extent that Medicaid is, you have to ask why the states have so much say in determining who gets what.

We should all agree that able-bodied individuals are accountable for themselves. If you're able-bodied and temporarily disadvantaged due to uncontrollable circumstances, then the government should provide support. I don't believe that level of support should be as high as that attainable by an able-bodied individual who's not disadvantaged. Why? Because if you're temporarily disadvantaged, we should incentivize you to overcome that disadvantage as your circumstances permit.

And if you're permanently disabled or born into a situation in which you're at a systemic disadvantage, the level of support should be higher. That's both morally right and in everyone's interest.

I still believe that government support programs should be customizable at the local level to reflect community differences. Customize the programs locally, but set funding and define applicability federally. A societal safety net is a big-government idea that requires big-government funding. It follows that it also requires a big-government rollout. Localizing the safety net would require localized funding, but as with insurance pools, it's much more cost-effective to pool risk at the largest level.

Again, it's not politics. It's just math.

9. A BIMODAL APPROACH

We can't tear down the healthcare house we're living in now and then build a new one. We need someplace to live in between. That leads us to a bimodal approach: as we build our new system from scratch, we leave the old system running in parallel until people transition from one to the other.

Consider Uber's titration in the taxi sector. They didn't start by saying, "Hey, we've got some people who are interested in driving for Uber," followed by a phase two of, "Hey, we've got a downloadable application people looking for a ride can use," and a phase three of, "Hey, we figured out a way for riders to pay drivers!" That's not how you do it. I don't believe we can continue to try to transition a system through half-baked, point-specific approaches. Instead, we need to map out an end-to-end experience.

Uber showed up with a viable end-to-end product. It's certainly evolved through countless iterations, but the end-to-end process was there from the start. There is a reason why taxi companies that responded by introducing app approaches limited to scheduling rides couldn't keep up with Uber—it was a point solution versus an end-to-end platform solution.

The parallel in healthcare? Build the end-to-end care and coverage system.

That means everything must be created: the governance, the platform, the individual insurance marketplace, the incentives, the cross-industry expertise, the modernized experience, the 85-percent mandate. Only then do the patients begin to shift from the old to the new.

The transition needs to start with market inertia—beginning, I believe, as large employers begin to shift. They're driving the profit margins of the big insurance companies. When players such as Walmart and Pepsi say, "This is how we're doing things in the future," insurance companies will be forced to respond. Some of the largest employer stakeholders in the country are already coming together around initiatives like the Employer Health Innovation Roundtable

(EHIR), whose members include Apple, Disney, Facebook, Google, Walmart, Fidelity, and Tesla. Progressive insurers are already moving too, looking to drive new insurance models with the backing and support of their employer clients.

Combine the momentum generated by players like these committing to a new approach with providers making the shift to a new future, and you've got a pretty good formula for success.

There's no half pregnancy here, no sequence of half steps leading from the shallow to the deep end of the pool. That's a process that won't ever reach its intended outcome, as we've seen with the insurance self-reform of value-based care.

THERE'S NO HALFWAY

The time for incremental reform has passed. We've spent years in pursuit of halfway solutions, and we've failed to deliver the results we all want to see. We need to shift from an old system to a new one. It's that simple and that powerful.

There can be no glide path involved here. Remember, a glide path is how you land a plane.

We're talking about taking off.

CONCLUSION

"The reasonable man adapts himself to the world: the unreasonable one persists in trying to adapt the world to himself. Therefore all progress depends on the unreasonable man."

—PLAYWRIGHT GEORGE BERNARD SHAW

Insurance companies have been given a long time to diagnose the failings of our (im)perfect system and not only set us on a path toward higher-quality outcomes and lower costs, but actually realize them. I've talked at length about their efforts to self-reform. However well intended these efforts might be, healthcare costs remain unsustainable. New jobs are added on top of old ones. The burden on employers who pay the bulk of the bill continues to grow, and millions of Americans remain one medical emergency away from bankruptcy. And we're still not getting the levels of health and wellness we're paying for.

Enough is enough.

What are we waiting for? How much worse does it have to get before we all feel compelled to act? There's never going to be a perfect political window. We either need to yank the window open now and head off the full-blown crisis that's coming, or we wait until the hurricane hits, shatters the window, and leaves us no choice at all.

It's time to be unreasonable. And I hope I've encouraged you to be just that.

I believe insurance companies should and will serve an essential role in this new system. As critical as I've been about their self-reform efforts, no other entity is better positioned to serve as an agent of the change that we need. So much good can come from the scale and expertise of the insurance sector—*if* carriers are willing to collaborate and prioritize their ethics and morals over their profits and margins. I know the insurance industry is filled with good people who want to do the right thing. I ask those good people to act on those instincts. Ask why things are the way they are. Then ask why again and again and again. Don't stop until you understand the issues at their core.

It won't be easy. The system is seemingly set up to be hard to understand and even harder to change. You will encounter pitfalls. You will run into things that don't make sense. You will find situations where the largest healthcare providers and the largest insurance companies resist real change because the status quo is serving them well. You will even find stakeholders you never knew of profiting off the current state of affairs. It is certain to seem that you can't fix everything, and sometimes you'll feel that you can't fix even the smallest thing either.

All this is necessary. If you don't find yourself in these situations, it means you're not digging deep enough. It means you're not yet the fully unreasonable man or woman we need to bring a better system into being—the kind of better system we all need and deserve.

Remember this mess is human made. That means it can be human solved.

It's silly for us to sit back and accept what is a human-made system that benefits the few, not the many. Human-made problems are much easier to address than the real insurmountable barriers our clinical teams are faced with every day. Let's not treat health insurance as a new form of metastasizing cancer. There's nothing inevitable about our healthcare system. Humans made the decisions to create the incentives, laws, regulations, and organizations that govern it.

We can fix it.

The elements of a better system aren't mysteries. They're known. Many have already been tried in fragmentary and isolated ways. Our challenge isn't so much discovery as it is momentum.

When you find a problem, raise it up. When you see an opportunity, announce it. It's never been easier for people who are determined to make a change to find, connect, and support each other. Ask why. Ask why not. Use your company message boards and continue to reach beyond the walls in which you work through other forms of social media.

How will we find each other? Let's try this:

#RichandDying

I'll start the conversation on LinkedIn—find my personal page or join the group named "Rich & Dying" that's dedicated to the discussion of this book and implementing real change. Let's all use the hashtag for posts that relate to solving this very solvable issue.

I look forward to finding you, hearing from you, and working with you. Ours is an essential cause. Let's be unreasonable—together.

ACKNOWLEDGMENTS

First, thanks to all my colleagues and acquaintances who are fighting the good fight! I've struggled, honestly, to strike a balance in this book between the provocative case that I believe circumstances demand with my respect and appreciation for the terrific people within the industry. Many of my friends and colleagues are involved in industry initiatives that I've found fault with. I want to make clear, once more, that the people in the insurance industry are one of its great strengths. To that I'd add that the efforts I've criticized aren't wasted efforts. They've taught us important lessons. But they haven't provided the sustainable answer, the affordable, high-quality healthcare system that Americans need and deserve. I see parallels in America's early struggles with space exploration, which served to fuel an extraordinary national commitment that brought astronauts to the moon in less than a decade. It's failure that brings us to the point where we choose to think bigger and more boldly—to not just reach into space but to reach for the moon, for Mars, and beyond.

To my friend, Mark, thank you for your assistance in getting these wild perspectives and ideas down on paper. Your professional yet personal approach has left a mark on me.

To my friends, family, and mentors, thanks for encouraging me to be an eternal student and supporting me in all the ways that you do. To my father, who taught me the value of thinking outside the box; my mother, who taught me the value of writing; and my stepfather, the value of reading. I owe a great deal of my discipline and desire to publish this book to each of you. And to my wife, you have taught me more than you'll ever know. It is because of you that I felt compelled to chase such a crazy idea.

And to you, the reader, if you've gotten this far, then I am grateful. That tells me you care about the same problems I do. I hope the book was as valuable for you as your interest makes it for me.

ABOUT THE AUTHOR

JEB DUNKELBERGER is the author of over one hundred publications related to improving the healthcare sector. He holds health-related degrees from Virginia Tech, London School of Economics and Political Science, London School of Hygiene & Tropical Medicine, Cornell University, and the University of Pennsylvania.

Jeb has intertwined his academic theories and perspectives with a mission-oriented professional life. After starting as a management consultant at Ernst & Young, Jeb served as a vice president in two of the nation's largest healthcare companies: Highmark, Inc. and McKesson Corp. Jeb's passions and energy took him to Silicon Valley, where he worked with Cricket Health, a value-based renal care provider, and Notable Health, an intelligent clinical automation company. Jeb now serves as the CEO of Sutter Health | Aetna, a Bay area payer-provider organization focused on delivering high-quality care through sustainably affordable health insurance products.

Jeb's personal mission is to help recognize and eradicate critical inefficiencies throughout the US healthcare economy while creating a group of similar-minded professionals to build the future of healthcare together.